Theories
of the
Bargaining
Process

Theories of the Bargaining Process

ALAN CODDINGTON
Foreword G.L.S. Shackle

AldineTransaction
A Division of Transaction Publishers
New Brunswick (U.S.A.) and London (U.K.)

First paperback printing 2007
Copyright © 1968 by George Allen & Unwin Ltd.

This book is printed on acid-free paper that meets the American National Standard for Permanence of Paper for Printed Library Materials.

Library of Congress Catalog Number: 2006048006
ISBN: 978-0-202-30917-0
Printed in the United States of America

Library of Congress Cataloging-in-Publication Data

Coddington, Alan.
    Theories of the bargaining process / Alan Coddington ; foreword by
G.L.S. Schackle.
            p. cm.
    Originally published: Chicago : Aldine Pub. Co., 1968.
    Includes bibliographical references and index.
    ISBN 978-0-202-30917-0 (alk. paper)
    1. Monopolies. I. Title.

HD2731.C6   2007
338.8'—dc22

                                                2006048006

FOREWORD

by Professor G. L. S. Shackle

The behaviour of inanimate objects is not governed by their possession or non-possession of conscious knowledge. It follows that in assimilating the behaviour of a society to that of an inanimate system, economists of the mechanistic school have assumed away the problem of what men can and cannot know and the influence on their conduct of the beliefs and assumptions, right or wrong, realisable or inherently self-defeating, with which they complement their knowledge or by which they develop proxies for the unknowable. When a type of situation or process presents itself, whose essence is the exploitation by one party of the ignorance of another, it is plain that mechanistic models, and even the scheme of *equilibrium*, designed to make conceivable the possession by every man of all the knowledge which the scheme makes useful to him, cannot dissect the heart of things.

Not ignorance and uncertainty merely, but mistakenness, belief in something which in fact is false, and further, the deliberate cultivation of uncertainty and mistakenness by one party in the mind of the other, are of the essence of bargaining. Orthodox economic analysis proceeds by saying: It would pay this individual best, in such-and-such circumstances, did he but know that those *are* his circumstances, to do so-and-so, let us assume that he does know and that he will do it. Equilibrium is the means of being able, without impediment of logic, to ascribe to him that complete relevant knowledge of his circumstances, without which he cannot demonstrate to himself that one course out of all possible courses is objectively the best. But when our problem, of its nature and by its essential terms, precludes us from ascribing to the individual this complete relevant knowledge, how is the economic analyst to proceed? He may content himself with rather general propositions, such as the insufficiency of the existence of a contract zone (within which any agreement, once reached, is better for *both* parties than no agreement) as a condition guaranteeing that an agreement *will* be reached; or the proposition that a contract zone need not leave the actual agreement indeterminate. These two propositions seem worth having, if nothing more can be attained, and they can be established[1] from rather general and basic considerations. But Dr Coddington has shown that much more can be attained, at a price.

A need is felt by many analysts to escape from the assumption that an *achieved optimum* is the only thing we can understand. How in detail, by what precise sequence of steps or flow of transformation, is a new such optimum attained when the governing conditions which shaped an earlier one have been destroyed? Is there necessarily a path which inevitably leads to a new adjustment? What can the effect be, when different parts of the system respond with various lags to disequilibrium pressures? Such questions lead to the search for principles determining the path of movement which a system will follow, to the devising of dynamic models characterised by equations which associate with each other events or situations of distinct dates. However, it seems that the determining of an equilibrium situation or state of affairs calls for far fewer arbitrary assumptions than that of a path of movement. The former essentially requires us to assume that people seek to satisfy tastes which are characterised by diminishing marginal rates of substitution, by means of resources which show diminishing marginal productivities; and that they possess all the knowledge of their own responses and the technological powers of their resources, and of each other's tastes, powers and intentions, which bears upon their own problems of choice. These are very general and,

[1] *Expectations in Economics*, Cambridge University Press, 1949, pp. 101–108.

except the last, very plausible assumptions. But no comparable appeal to the basic qualities of human nature and the basic geometry, as it were, of technology can be invoked to select one particular path of movement out of an infinity of such paths. If such a model as Dr Coddington has constructed is to be worth while, it must show itself capable of illustrating and exemplifying principles much more general than its particular illustration of them, such as could scarcely otherwise be elicited. This, I think, is the claim that Dr Coddington's model can make.

What Dr Coddington has essentially studied is the nature of consistency in a bargainer's system of expectations and intentions. Dr Coddington's model eschews the problem of uncertainty, and the expectations which his bargainer entertains at any 'now' are single-valued, one value only of each variable being assigned to each calendar date which is still in the future. As the bargainer's present moment moves along the calendar axis, these assigned values are successively tested. Since there are several variables, there is for each date a vector of values assigned to that date. *Consistency over time* is present in an individual's system of expectations and intentions, if the fulfilment of expectations concerning variables which he does not control will lead to his maintaining unchanged the actions he has proposed for himself for the date in question. The study of this problem cannot attain clear results except in a rather simple and specific model. It is such a model that Dr Coddington has devised, and its value lies in its exposing questions and difficulties, about the logic of expectation and decision in a bargaining situation, which would otherwise have remained concealed in the fog of elusiveness and complexity which this intensely difficult theme engenders.

Consistency over time is a possible character of a single individual's expectations. It consists in his needing to make no change of plan so long as his expectations continue to prove to have been right. But what are the conditions which will make them prove right? Dr Coddington shows that 'Stackelberg disequilibrium' is as much a feature of the bargaining situation as of the context of its original discovery, the duopoly situation. All the theories of bargaining, which he surveys, *essentially* involve mistakenness on the part of one or both bargainers about the decision-rule that will be adopted by the other. Thus the search for a settlement, according to any of these theories and Dr Coddington's own, must consist in a series of revelations and attempted corrections of error, the precise description of the specific process in any instance depending on an *arbitrary* choice of initial decision-rule. Dr Coddington's achievement is to have brought some essential aspects of such a process into the light by constructing, with exemplary precision and clarity, some models sufficiently specified to enable their consequences to be computed and described in detail.

The impression made upon a critically attentive reader by Dr Coddington's argument is that of a natural and incisive professionalism and the rarest kind of intellectual high efficiency. His problem is of the utmost subtlety and complexity, a tangled thicket of difficulties and distractions. He has not been distracted. Drastic selection, abstraction, simplification and specification have served to clear some fresh and solid ground. The capacity to limit one's aims to what can be made completely clear, precise and capable of proof, when no more is needed for his overall strategic purpose, is a mark of high generalship.

CONTENTS

PREFACE

Microeconomic theory has been almost exclusively concerned with the workings of competition within different forms of market. Even the theories of pure monopoly and pure monopsony presuppose the existence of competition on one side of the market. But the question naturally arises as to what happens when competition is absent on both sides of the market. Such a situation is termed bilateral monopoly and has been traditionally regarded by economists as 'indeterminate'. But to label the situation indeterminate is to confuse theory with reality. For it is the theory which is indeterminate, not the situation. A theory which considers only the competitive structure of market situations will obviously leave the outcome unexplained within wide limits when competition is entirely absent. But the methodological implication of this is not that the outcome is unexplainable. On the contrary, the implication is that the outcome is in need of explanation. The situation therefore provides an invitation to introduce additional factors into the theoretical framework. Such is the methodological basis for a theory of the bargaining process as an explanation of the conditions of exchange under bilateral monopoly.

Like the theory of perfect competition, the theory of 'perfect' bilateral monopoly may be seen as a polar extreme. Even if a perfectly competitive market has never existed, the theory of perfect competition is relevant, as a useful analytical simplification, to situations where competition is abundant. Similarly, one may argue that the theory of bilateral monopoly is relevant to situations where competition is limited. J. K. Galbraith's account of American capitalism in terms of the concept of countervailing power[1] may be seen as an attempt to substitute a bilateral monopoly-inspired model for the classical competitive model; it may be seen as an attempt to bring the idea of bargaining power from the periphery of economic theory to the very centre.

The theory of games has been widely regarded as the appropriate framework of analysis when competition is limited and individual decisions have significant effects on the outcome of the process. More generally, game theory has been presented as *the* theory of interdependent decision-making processes. However, although game theory has given rise to new and elegant ways of formulating and systematising these problems, it does not seem to have yielded much in the way of new predictions and explanations. This is particularly apparent in the case of bilateral monopoly. As S. A. Ozga has written: 'The most obvious field for the application of the theory [of games] to economics is that of oligopoly and bilateral monopoly. Even in this case, however, little more has been achieved so far than the presentation of some parts of the existing theory in game theoretic terms'.[2]

This is not to say that the theory of games has no relevance to the social sciences. It may indeed serve as an indispensable starting point for posing a problem and revealing the essential issues involved, and it has certainly had practical uses within, for example, social psychology, as a framework for gaming experiments. These uses are, however, distinct from the generation of theoretical propositions. In any case, the theory of games has made the greatest theoretical progress in the sphere of constant-sum games—a sphere which is uninteresting from the point of view of economics and irrelevant to the understanding of bilateral monopoly. Bilateral monopoly is not a constant-sum game. And the application of game theory to variable-sum

[1] J. K. Galbraith, *American Capitalism: The Concept of Countervailing Power*, Hamish Hamilton, London, 1957.

[2] S. A. Ozga, *Expectations in Economic Theory*, Weidenfeld and Nicolson, London, 1965, p. 262.

situations tends to produce a map of all the possibilities (enlightening though this may be for some purposes), rather than a theory of what is likely to happen. It is my own view that game theory has been pitched on too high a level of generality to provide a fruitful framework for theoretical investigations of a particular kind of situation like bilateral monopoly.

It seems appropriate to make some mention of the methodological assumptions implicit in this work. In embarking on an extravaganza of mathematical model-building one faces a great danger of becoming so intrigued and enchanted with the workings of the models that one loses all contact with reality. This is the principal hazard of finding a model which 'works'— one may become totally enamoured with one's own creation. However, bearing in mind this danger, the very activity of model building can be analytically therapeutic in various ways, particularly when the models collapse or yield absurd results. In setting up the formal schemes one is forced to think more clearly about the factors, structures and mechanisms involved in the problem. It becomes necessary to isolate the assumptions which cause a model to behave in an absurd or unrealistic way. And in spelling out explicit models one is less likely to drift into the semantic quagmire which results from the confusion of theoretical concepts with the real world phenomena to which they supposedly correspond. However, it is always important to remember that although a formal scheme may facilitate thought within its own framework, it may also constrain subsequent thought to remain within that framework. The danger of the reification of formal schemes and models is always present.

A more difficult methodological problem is the question of the empirical content of the models. This is where mathematical model building is particularly vulnerable to criticism. For it is one thing to build a model which 'works', but it is quite a different thing to establish a correspondence between the components of the model and particular aspects of the real world. The danger here is that of lapsing into various forms of illusion—of imagining that the precision of the formalism entails a corresponding accuracy of the theory in its relation to the world (or, even worse, that the very fact of formalisation lends authority to the assumptions underlying it). On reflection, it is clear that a formal (or any other) theory can only have accuracy in so far as its components can be identified in reality. And this is a question quite distinct from, and independent of, the precision of the formalism.

The question of whether a model has empirical content seems to hinge on whether its components can be identified *ex ante*, or whether they can only be brought into the picture *ex post*. If a theory can only be applied to an event *ex post* we might say that it provides an interpretation rather than an explanation of the event. For example, if one bargainer does better than a second in a particular bargaining process and we attribute this to the greater bargaining skill of the first, the question arises as to how we recognise bargaining skill. If this can only be identified after the event by observing who does better in the bargaining process, then the concept of bargaining skill has no explanatory value. Saying that a bargainer had greater bargaining skill would merely be another way of saying that he was the one who did better in the process. In this very crude example we could say that the bargaining skill theory had no empirical content.

Too much should not be read into this point. It is not being argued that *ex post* interpretations are devoid of meaning, but only that they lack empirical content. It would be quite cavalier to dismiss them as worthless for the tasks of theorising, for an interpretation may indeed be the embryo of a theory. An *ex post* interpretation can be the source of insights which play an indispensable heuristic part in the development of subsequent theory. Thus, it must be stressed that what we are concerned with here is simply empirical content and not some wider notion of theoretical fruitfulness.

There are two ways in which the empirical content of a

model may be established, in this context: (*a*) the components of the model (i.e. in mathematical models, the parameters) may, in principle at least, be identified independently of the bargaining process in question. In this way the observation of a sequence of bargaining processes might provide the basis for an explanation of subsequent bargaining processes. (It appears that econometric models have empirical content in this first sense.)

(*b*) The components of the model might be identified, in principle at least, independently of bargaining behaviour. This is evidently a much stronger criterion of empirical content than the former one. We might illustrate this second criterion as follows. Suppose a bargaining model is composed of parameters relating to the learning and discounting behaviour of each bargainer, and suppose further that these parameters could be established, in principle at least, by confronting each bargainer with certain standard situations not involving his interaction with the other bargainer. Such a model would then have empirical content according to our second criterion. It would certainly constitute more than an *ex post* interpretation of the bargaining process.

This second type of theory would amount to a reduction of the phenomenon to explanation in terms of the propensities of individuals. Although it would be quite wrong to suppose that such a type of theory is necessary for progress in a field, or constitutes the only genuine explanation of a social phenomenon, the models examined in this work are essentially of this second type. They can therefore be said to have empirical content in this second sense. It is important to note, in passing, that the question of the empirical content of a theory is quite distinct from the question of its correspondence with the world. The first can be established in principle (by showing the theory to be non-tautological), whereas the second can only be established in practice.

The activity of attempting to assess the truth of a theory is commonly referred to as 'empirical testing'. There is currently a widespread view that empirical testing is a good thing. However, the unqualified clamour for such activity often arises from an uncritical view of the nature of economic facts. For if theory and fact are in conflict it means that the theory is wrong or the facts are wrong (or possibly both). The view that theory must always give way to facts,[1] characteristic of the latter-day methodologists who maintain the urgency of empirical testing of theories, rests on a particular view of facts as hard gritty things which litter the world waiting to be picked up. This view of economic facts is quite insupportable. Since the world is composed of situations (which may be described in varying degrees of adequacy by facts) the facts that we have at our disposal have been created, not found. They have been created, furthermore, only within a conceptual framework which has involved selecting some aspects of the situations we find in the world. A typical economic fact (e.g. as found in the National Income Blue Book) is itself the outcome of the application of various theories, concepts and judgements. It has been created only with great difficulty and is subject to a host of errors and uncertainties which we cannot even begin to enumerate here. It is therefore quite misleading to regard facts, in economics, as some kind of raw sense data, beyond dispute and revision. One does not go out onto the Treasury steps and observe the domestic level of economic activity. Facts need testing, as do theories. What is at one time regarded as a fact may well be contradicted by subsequent evidence. There may even be widespread disagreement as to which evidence is relevant and whether a given piece of evidence should be interpreted as supporting or undermining the original fact. To the historian, this view is so commonplace as to verge on the banal. But it is a view towards which the economic theorist, in his methodological reflections at any rate, shows a great aversion.[1]

[1] R. G. Lipsey's influential textbook ends on this note: '. . . as scientists we must always remember that, when theory and fact come into conflict, it is theory, not fact, that must give way.' R. G. Lipsey, *Introduction to Positive Economics* (Second Edition), Weidenfeld and Nicolson, London, 1966, p. 859.

The relevance to the present work of this digression is that data of sufficient quality to use in formal testing of theories of the bargaining process do not seem to exist at the present. It is also doubtful whether such data could be collected within the context of existing institutions and research techniques.

The foregoing is not intended as an argument that the only equipment needed to push back the frontiers of economics is an armchair and a pipe. On the contrary, when it comes to fighting last year's battles, I would side with the view that any substantive discipline advances by the interplay of theory and experience. For the present, however, it would seem more important to help moderate the positivist excesses of the victors by arguing that this interplay is a subtle process, not a one-way bulldozing of theories by unassailable facts.

In the light of this discussion, the methodological position taken here may be summed up as follows. Although there are no data sufficiently rich or reliable to test the theories in any formal way, nevertheless there are certain broad features of bargaining processes which are well known (e.g. a bargaining process sometimes leads to an agreement but sometimes to a breakdown of the negotiations). To make a start, we need theories which can account for these broad outlines (or, 'stylised facts', in the jargon). Whether a theory can explain the well-known broad features of the process can be thought of as a rather weak test of the theory. In this way one has an interplay between theory and reality on a very general level. Does the model behave in a plausible way? It must be admitted that such a test is a relatively weak one. But, on the other hand, it seems singularly pointless, at this stage of the development of the theory of bargaining processes, to devise severe tests (even supposing appropriate facts could be assembled) which the theories would almost undoubtedly fail. One of the problems of the interplay of theory and fact lies in the choosing of tests appropriate to the stage of development of the theory and to the stage of development of the facts. When the broad features have received a theoretical explanation and when data of some quality becomes available, then the time will be ripe for performing tests which are more severe.

This book is the result of study which was undertaken while I was the holder, successively, of the Sir Ellis Hunter Memorial Scholarship and the Sir Ellis Hunter Memorial Fellowship at the University of York. I would like to express my sincere appreciation for the advice and encouragement of my supervisors at York, Professor Alan T. Peacock and Dr John H. Williamson. I am also indebted to Mr Brian Phillips, of the University of Leeds Computing Laboratory, who wrote the program used in computing solutions to the set of equations in Chapter VI, and to Dr Jeremy R. Ravetz, of the University of Leeds Philosophy Department, with whom I engaged in countless discussions of all manner of things connected with this study. The inadequacies of the work are, however, entirely my own responsibility.

Chapter I

THE GENERAL FRAMEWORK

'The process of reorganization of economic images through messages is the key to the understanding of economic dynamics.'

Kenneth E. Boulding[1]

1. INTRODUCTION

Concerning social action, Talcott Parsons has made the following observation:

'It is a fundamental property of action . . . that it does not consist only of ad hoc "responses" to particular situational "stimuli" but that the actor develops a *system* of "expectations" relative to the various objects of the situation. These *may* be structured only relative to his own need-dispositions and the probabilities of gratification or deprivation contingent on the various alternatives of action which he may undertake. But in the case of interaction with social objects a further dimension is added. Part of ego's expectation, in many cases the most crucial part, consists in the probable *re*action of alter to ego's possible action, a reaction which comes to be anticipated in advance and thus to affect ego's own choices'.[2]

The present work may be seen as an attempt to explore this property of social action within a particular economic context.

---

[1] K. E. Boulding, *The Image*, University of Michigan Press, Ann Arbor, 1961, p. 90.
[2] T. Parsons, *The Social System*, Free Press of Glencoe, New York, 1951, p. 5.

1

2. THE CONCEPT OF AN ECONOMIC ENVIRONMENT

In the theory of markets it has been possible to deal theoretically with the interaction of many economic actors by supposing that each one acts in an 'environment' characterised by some representation of the aggregate behaviour of all the remaining actors. What is meant here by an environment is a theoretical construction which serves to represent, for each actor, the behaviour of all the relevant economic units which are not under his immediate control. It is clear that it is in general neither theoretically possible nor conceptually useful to consider separately the interaction between every pair of economic units. Hence, the construction of economic environments exhibiting various forms of behaviour results, in some cases, in a considerable clarification of the nature of the individual decision-making processes which underlie the behaviour of different market forms.

This approach to microeconomics has been particularly enlightening in circumstances involving a large number of economic units. It is well known, however, that processes involving only a small number of economic units pose many theoretical problems which arise from the much stronger interdependence of the actors in these circumstances. Attempts have been made to deal theoretically with these processes in terms of much the same environment concepts as proved fruitful in the case of many economic units.[1] Alternatively, the application of game theory to these problems has put much greater stress on the strategic reasoning involved in individual decision-making under such conditions of interdependence.

In the present work we wish to approach a particularly

[1] See E. H. Chamberlin, *The Theory of Monopolistic Competition*, 7th edition, Harvard University Press, Cambridge, Mass., 1956; W. J. Fellner, *Competition Among the Few*, Knopf, New York, 1949; R. Triffin, *Monopolistic Competition and General Equilibrium Theory*, Harvard University Press, Cambridge, Mass., 1940.

2

simple small group process—two-person bargaining. In a situation of bilateral monopoly there is observed, rather than the straightforward trading characteristic of competitive markets, what Edgeworth referred to as 'the characteristic evil of indeterminate contract, *deadlock*, undecidable opposition of interests' and 'the tendency . . . towards dissimulation and objectionable arts of higgling'.[1] According to Edgeworth, economic theory is quite innocent of these objectionable arts. Subsequent writers have dissented from this view, as will become apparent.

We will approach the theory of the bargaining process here from the point of view of individual decision-making, although the decision-making model will be of the simple utility maximising rather than the game theory type in which the treatment of the interdependence of maximising processes is much more explicit. The interdependence will still arise but via a theory of expectations and their adjustment. Furthermore, in order to add more structure to the model than the bare system of payoffs characteristic of the game theory approach, we wish to work within the spirit of the environment concepts characteristic of the theories dealing with large group processes. So we will be concerned here with the construction of systems of actions to represent the expected responses of a single actor to the decision-maker's possible actions (rather than, as has been the more characteristic use of such environment concepts, to represent the responses of an aggregate of actors to the decision-maker's actions). As the work of J. G. Cross has shown,[2] this type of approach allows one to take the emphasis away from strategic reasoning within a static framework in order to look at the sequential aspects of the process of action and re-action taking place within the bargaining situation.

---

[1] F. Y. Edgeworth, *Mathematical Psychics*, C. Kegan Paul, London, 1881, pp. 29–30.

[2] J. G. Cross, 'A Theory of the Bargaining Process,' Ph.D. thesis, Princeton University, Princeton, 1964; J. G. Cross, 'A Theory of the Bargaining Process,' *American Economic Review*, 55, 1965, pp. 67–94.

3

3. A BARGAINING SITUATION

To illustrate in a more concrete way the contrast between the theoretical approaches which are appropriate to large group processes on the one hand and small group processes on the other, we consider a monopolist facing first a group of many buyers[1] and second a monopsonist. When the monopolist faces a market involving many actors, he may regard the responses of this complex and finely structured environment to his own pricing decisions as quite adequately represented by a demand curve. For any price which the monopolist chooses, he expects the environment to respond by buying a certain quantity of his output. However, when the monopolist is faced with a monopsonist, he is no longer concerned with an aggregate response to his decisions. And when the aggregate disappears so too does the statistical regularity which can be generated by a sufficiently large group of actors. The monopolist faces another decision-maker. We have arrived at the old economic problem of the theory of bilateral monopoly or 'isolated exchange'.

As Siegel and Fouraker point out, the situation of bilateral monopoly has a significance which extends beyond the immediate economic context:

'. . . the bare structure of the situation has the essential characteristics of many social conflict situations. In one sense, a situation of bilateral monopoly appeals to the mutual interests of the participants, and would seem to call for harmonious cooperation between them. In another, the interests of the participants are exactly in opposition, and acrimonious competition would seem to be the behaviour norm. Social scientists are particularly concerned with the system of decisions whereby such conflicts are resolved'.[2]

[1] Whenever the phrase 'many buyers' is used it is implied that no one buyer has any control over the market price.

[2] S. Siegel and L. E. Fouraker, *Bargaining and Group Decision Making*, McGraw-Hill, New York, 1960, p. 1.

Thus we may wish to see bilateral monopoly as the paradigm of a wider class of social situations involving both mutuality and opposition of interests.

To return to the previous theme, we can see that when the monopolist faces a monopsonist rather than a group of many buyers, he will expect a different form of response to his decisions. The monopsonist, since he has a significant control over the group behaviour, is in a position not just to buy or not (as the individuals in the group of many buyers were), but also to *bargain*. Thus, in connection with each transaction, the monopolist expects not just a single response, but a response which extends into the future.

In elementary theory the demand curve associated with many buyers is taken as fixed and known to the monopolist. However, as greater realism is brought into the theory, we must admit that monopolists do not usually know the exact form of the demand curve. Therefore, with the development of the theory of monopoly, it is necessary to consider adjustments over time, i.e. the processes by which present decisions depend on previous responses of the environment.[1]

When we come to bilateral monopoly, on the other hand, it seems that the fact that each actor does not know in advance the exact form of the other's response is fundamental to the workings of the process. The loss of the relative stability of aggregate behaviour now gives rise to a wider range of possible responses. So we are led to argue that the adjustment of expectations regarding responses is an important factor in the process. (As we shall see in Chapter IV, there are in any case theoretical objections to the assumption that expectations are fulfilled.) Consequently, any theory of the dynamics of the bargaining process which fails to take account of this should be regarded as seriously inadequate. This brings us to a consideration of the process in which a series of demands and counter-demands leads either to an agreement or a breakdown of the bargaining.

[1] See, for example, H. Wold, (ed.), *Econometric Model Building*, North Holland Publishing Co., Amsterdam, 1964.

Such a process is the means by which the conditions of exchange are typically determined within a situation of bilateral monopoly. Thus, an understanding of the workings of this kind of process would seem a fruitful basis for the development of the theory of bilateral monopoly.

What we wish to consider is whether the concept of an economic environment can be enriched sufficiently to allow an analysis of the kind of decisions which are involved in this two-person process. In attempting to show that this is possible, we shall, in the following sections, develop what is essentially a system of responses which each bargainer can use to represent the behaviour of the other bargainer. This is closely analogous in principle to the way the behaviour of a group of many buyers can be represented by a demand curve (or system of conditional responses) although the representation will be rather more elaborate in the case of the two-person bargaining process.

4. FORMALISATION

A bargaining situation may be represented quite generally by the following elements:

(1) a pair of variables q_1, q_2, representing the demands of the two bargainers at any point in time. (If each party to the bargaining process is an organisation rather than a single person, we suppose here that it acts in a perfectly coordinated way regarding its choice of a demand q_i. Any problems concerning the internal consensus of either organisation, or of intra-organisational bargaining, are neglected in this study. For a discussion of these problems see R. E. Walton and R. B. McKersie, *A Behavioral Theory of Labor Negotiations*, McGraw-Hill, New York, 1965, Chapters VIII and IX);

(2) a pair of utility functions $u_1(q_1)$, $u_2(q_2)$ with $u_1'(q_1) > 0$ and $u_2'(q_2) > 0$, representing the preferences of the two bargainers among the possible agreements;

(3) a fixed amount M such that disagreement between the bargainers occurs if $q_1 + q_2 > M$. Here it is supposed that M,

6

which may be thought of as representing the total product available for sharing between the two bargainers, is a parameter of the situation. However, it may be that, especially in the longer run, the two bargainers can collaborate to increase the total product. Thus, a possibility which is not considered in the present work is that the bargainers may devote their energies to increasing the size of M rather than each trying to increase his own share of M. This possibility is discussed by Walton and McKersie under the heading of 'Integrative Bargaining'.[1] We define $q_1 = 0$ to be the point which represents, for bargainer 1, the 'no agreement' outcome and similarly $q_2 = 0$ represents the 'no agreement' outcome for bargainer 2. Since even a cardinal utility function is determined only up to positive linear transformations, we are free to choose the utility functions such that $u_1(0) = 0$, $u_2(0) = 0$. This formalisation is represented in Figure 1.1. The horizontal line AB is of length M. The variable q_1 is measured from A to B and the variable q_2 is measured from B to A. Thus any point along AB is a point at which $q_1 + q_2 = M$ and therefore a possible point of agreement. The position of the zero point for bargainer 1 will depend on what happens to him if there is no agreement. Thus, if he is threatened by bargainer 2 with dire consequences in the event of no agreement, this may, in terms of Figure 1.1, shift the point $q_1 = 0$ to the left. Thus when a (constant) cloud of mutual threats hangs over the bargaining process, this is reflected by the positions of the points A, B in Figure 1.1. This formalisation excludes the possibility of the announcement of a new threat during the course of the bargaining. We confine our attention to 'fixed threat' bargaining, which of course includes the case where threats are completely absent. If threats are absent, the points of disagreement and the *status quo* points coincide.

The interpretation of this formalisation is that all the possible agreements can be arranged in an order from A to B such that bargainer 1 always prefers agreements closer to B while bargainer 2 always prefers agreements closer to A. We have assumed

[1] Walton and McKersie, *op. cit.* pp. 126–83.

7

that the two bargainers have strictly opposing interests through-out the range of possible agreements, or contract zone, *AB*. A simple example of such a situation would occur if two bargainers were to share £*M* between them, the actual shares to be decided by mutual agreement. Any pair of numbers (representing the claims of the bargainers) which adds up to *M* is a possible agree-ment and whenever the pair adds to greater than *M* there is disagreement. Thus, within this formalism, we confine our

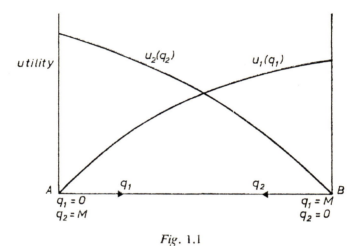

Fig. 1.1

attention to the processes involved in the determination of the value of a variable which has the following properties: first, that it is in the common interest of two decision-makers to agree to a value within some interval (the contract zone); second, that within this interval there is a direct clash of inter-ests between the decision-makers regarding the size of the variable. Bilateral monopoly then emerges as a special case of this framework if we suppose that all the outcomes considered by the two participants can be arranged in a list such that one prefers outcomes higher up the list while the other prefers outcomes lower down. This involves the assumption that the considered outcomes consist of only some of the set of all possible outcomes, namely those from which no mutually

8

advantageous adjustments can be made at the time of agreement. It then follows that there are diametrically opposed interests over the considered outcomes.

Cross, in the abstract of his Ph.D. thesis, speaks of his model involving only 'Pareto optimal outcome possibilities', but this is a source of some confusion and ambiguity. For since both bargainers prefer agreements sooner than later, an outcome would only be Pareto optimal as viewed from the start of the process if it were achieved immediately. Cross, however, is presumably concerned with Pareto optimality as viewed from

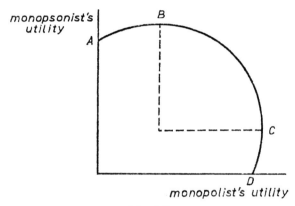

Fig. 1.2

the moment of agreement, which is a very different matter. We can refer to this as Pareto optimality in the small. It then transpires that Pareto optimality in the small is not a very significant concept in the present context since an agreement which is not Pareto optimal in the small may be Pareto preferred in the large (i.e. when viewed from the start of the process) to a second agreement which is Pareto optimal in the small. This would occur if the second agreement took sufficiently longer to achieve than the first. Thus, there are different senses of Pareto optimality depending on the point in time from which one views the process and these different senses carry quite different significances.

9

Diagrammatically, if all possible outcomes are represented by a region $ABCD$ in Figure 1.2, then we suppose that the considered outcomes referred to above are those along the upper right frontier BC, since all movements from within $ABCD$ upwards and to the right would be mutually advantageous. Bargaining would then consist of the determination of the value of a variable which is defined along BC. The utilities in the diagram refer to preferences at the time of agreement.

Since a bargaining process consists of a series of demands and counter-demands leading to either agreement or breakdown, the variation of the demands q_1 and q_2 as the bargaining

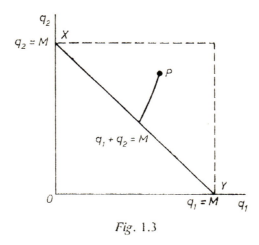

Fig. 1.3

proceeds may be represented by the motion of a point P in the q_1, q_2 plane, an agreement occurring if this point reaches the line $q_1 + q_2 = M$ (shown as XY in Figure 1.3). For a bargaining situation to exist there must be disagreement initially, so we must start with the representative point, P, above and to the right of XY, expressing the inequality $q_1 + q_2 > M$.

5. INDETERMINACY

It is clear that the theoretical considerations advanced so far do not single out any one of the possible agreements as the one which is likely to occur. Faced with this situation, that the static economic structure allows a whole range of possible outcomes, many writers have declared that the outcome of bilateral monopoly is indeterminate.[1] However, as Pen has pointed out, it is not the outcome which is indeterminate but the theory.[2] This was quite apparent to Fellner when he wrote:

'For the implication of the statement that price and output are indeterminate in certain ranges is *not* that we should be agnostic about what is likely to happen within the ranges in question. The implications of such a statement are essentially methodological. The statement merely carries the suggestion that, after the establishment of a range of possible values, a different apparatus should be employed in the discussion of what is likely to happen within that range.'[3]

The existence of indeterminacy seems to imply that we cannot achieve a proper understanding of bilateral monopoly without introducing further concepts into the theoretical framework. In this way we are led to examine the bargaining process and hence to assemble a theoretical framework in which dynamic considerations are possible.

It is of interest to note that Bowley has shown that under special institutional arrangements the problem becomes determinate even within a static framework.[4] Under these arrangements one of the traders quotes a price and the other trader then decides how much he will buy or sell at that price. It will be seen that such an arrangement is a very special case. It can be shown,

---

[1] Pen (J. Pen, 'A General Theory of Bargaining,' *American Economic Review*, 42, 1952, p. 24) lists the following as subscribing to this view: Bohm-Bawerk, Bowley, A. M. Henderson, Marshall, Nichol, Pigou, Stackelberg, Stigler, Tintner.

[2] *Ibid.*

[3] W. J. Fellner, *Competition Among the Few*, Knopf, New York, 1959, p. 10.

[4] A. L. Bowley, 'On Bilateral Monopoly,' *Economic Journal*, 38, 1928, pp. 651-59.

furthermore, that under plausible assumptions regarding the forms of the functions involved, it is always advantageous to be the trader who quotes a price rather than the one who responds with a quantity decision.[1] Thus, since each participant has the power of veto, why should one of them accept an inherently disadvantageous role? The existence of such an arrangement would seem to raise questions which could only be answered by a more general theory of behaviour in bilateral monopoly situations. We shall see in Chapter II that subsequent writers have also attempted to develop theories of the bargaining process which are determinate even within a static framework.

6. EXPECTATIONS

As we have already mentioned, we wish to extend the theoretical framework by introducing expectations extending into the future. It is no longer sufficient to consider in the decision-making process the expectation of a single response in the absence of a time dimension. Each bargainer acts in accordance with his expectations of how the other bargainer will respond to his acts.[2] By setting this up in a formal way it may be possible to cast some light on what Fellner calls the 'conjectural interdependence' inherent in the process.[3]

In addition to this we also wish to consider the *adjustment* of expectations in these circumstances. As we have already pointed out, the responses of a single actor are not likely to possess the stability and hence predictability of an aggregate of individuals. We would expect then that the adjustment of expectations would be an important, even essential, aspect of the process. In order to incorporate such mechanisms into our account of the process,

[1] See S. Siegel and L. E. Fouraker, *Bargaining and Group Decision Making*, McGraw-Hill, New York, 1960, pp. 3–7.

[2] This idea may correspond to what Parsons has called the element of 'double contingency' involved in social interaction. T. Parsons, *The Social System*, Free Press of Glencoe, New York, 1951, p. 10.

[3] Fellner, *op. cit.* p. 14.

it can be supposed that, at any point in time, each bargainer believes that the other will respond to his decisions in a particular way. However, as the process continues, each may discover that his beliefs were mistaken. It should be made clear that we do not consider how a bargainer surveys, at any instant, all the mutually exclusive possibilities and selects from these a single possibility, or what is effectively a single possibility, as his expectation. That is to say, we do not come to grips with the problem of decision-making under uncertainty. Rather, we represent the effects of the bargainers' incomplete knowledge by assuming the existence of changing expectations, each one being held with complete confidence until it is revised.

7. GENERAL WORKINGS OF THE MODEL

We are now in a position to outline the mechanism by which the process evolves within this framework.

Suppose we start by considering one of the bargainers (bargainer 1). He will come to the bargainer process with certain initial expectations regarding bargainer 2's responses to his possible courses of action. These expectations may well turn out to be mistaken. Bargainer 1 also brings with him a set of preferences among the possible outcomes—where an outcome is thought of as a particular bargain at a particular point in time. Although he may prefer agreements which are, at the time of agreement, more favourable to him, he will also prefer agreements which are arrived at sooner to those arrived at later. He therefore chooses his own plan both from the point of view of the bargain to which he expects it to lead and from the point of view of the time at which he expects the agreement to take place. Therefore, with an initial set of expectations about the form of bargainer 2's bargaining behaviour, bargainer 1 may weigh up his own alternative possibilities and choose a plan which leads, from his own point of view, to the best outcome attainable in the (conjectured) circumstances.

He then puts this initial plan into action and makes his initial demand.

All this applies equally well to bargainer 2. He also has initial expectations regarding bargainer 1's behaviour and in the light of these he has also chosen his initial plan. However, the crucial point is that as soon as the bargaining begins each bargainer is in a position to test his initial expectations regarding the other's behaviour.

Suppose 1 makes his demand in the light of his initial expectations and then 2 makes his demand similarly. Bargainer 1 is

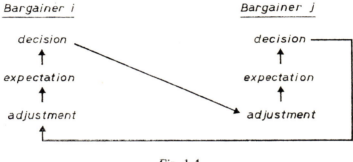

Fig. 1.4

then in a position to see exactly how bargainer 2 responded to his initial demand. This response may not be in accord with 1's initial expectations. If this is so then 1 must revise his expectations about 2's behaviour and in so doing he must revise his own plan. If it transpired that 1's expectations were fulfilled, then, of course, he would continue to put into action his initial plan. But if his expectations have been revised his second demand is made in accordance with a revised plan.

Now, from 2's point of view, this second demand of bargainer 1 (which could be the same as his first) constitutes 1's response to 2's initial demand. So now 2 can also test his initial expectations and revise them if necessary. If his expectations are revised this leads to a revised plan in the light of which his second demand is made. If his expectations are fulfilled his

14

second demand is made in the light of his initial plan. And so it goes on.

This mechanism is represented schematically in Figure 1.4. Starting at some arbitrary point in the proceedings we may trace the repercussions of a single decision round one cycle as follows:

(a) In the light of his current expectations, 1 chooses a plan and announces his current demand in accordance with this plan.

(b) This demand is noted by bargainer 2 who uses it to test his expectations about 1's behaviour. If his expectations are revised, he makes his current demand in the light of a revised plan. Otherwise he makes it in the light of his previously adopted current plan.

(c) 2's demand is noted by 1 and used to test his (1's) expectations regarding 2's behaviour. If his expectations are revised he makes his next demand in the light of a revised plan. Otherwise he makes it in the light of his current plan. The dynamics of the model then consist simply of a repetition of these cycles until such time (if any) as agreement is reached.

It can be seen, then, that the model can be divided into three parts: a theory of decision-making; a theory of expectations and a theory of the adjustment of expectations. Throughout the bulk of this work, a simple utility-maximisation theory of decision-making will be employed and only in the later discussion will the game theory model be mentioned. The problems involved in the development of a workable theory of expectations will be discussed in Chapter VI, and the relationship between expectations and decision-making will be examined in Chapter IV. The theory of the adjustment of expectations will not be seriously pursued in this work.

MATHEMATICAL APPENDIX

1. NOTATION

Our aim here is to develop a notation in which the idea of changing expectations may be expressed. First it is necessary to distinguish two kinds of time variable; present time, which we denote by T, and future time, which we denote by t. Present time is measured from a point which is fixed in history and is the time which actually elapses. It is the time which is registered on the calendar. Future time is measured from the present moment and is the dimension along which expectations extend. Rather than a particular date, it is a time 'so far hence'. Thus, future time 'elapses' only in the sense that one may be imagining what will happen at instants further and further into the future. Since we are interested, ultimately, in what actually happens rather than what is imagined will happen, we seek to reduce our theory eventually to functions depending on T and not on t.

The second distinction which we wish to make follows quite naturally from the first. This concerns the distinction between the value of a variable at some present time, T, and the expected value of a variable at some future time, t. The value of a variable we write simply as $q_i(T)$ where the subscript i refers to the bargainer whose current demand this is. The expected value of a variable, however, involves two subscripts, one referring to the bargainer who has the expectation and one referring to the bargainer whose demand the expectation concerns. Thus, we may write i's current expectation of the future variation of j's demand as $E_i(T)\{q_j(t)\}$. The presence of the variable T after the E refers to the fact that expectations will in general depend on present time. The presence of the variable t after the q refers to the fact that at any given time, T, the expectations will extend into the future. Thus, when $i \neq j$ the notation refers to a bargainer's expectation of the other's future behaviour and when

17

$i = j$ it refers to a bargainer's expectations of his own future behaviour (i.e. his plans).

It should become apparent in due course why this somewhat fanciful notation is called for by the present problem. However, it seems appropriate at this stage to point out the importance of notation in works of theory. Analysis is easily conditioned by the quality of the notation within which it is presented. When a theory is recast in an adequately developed notation, it is likely that new questions arise and new generalisations suggest themselves. This may be apparent when we come to reformulate the theory of Cross within the present notation. As one example of the role which notation can play, we may consider Cross's variable r_2 which is what bargainer 1 expects bargainer 2's concession rate to be. We know that this is a variable, but in Cross's notation we cannot tell whether it is a function of t but not of T, of T but not t, or of both t and T. In fact it transpires that in Cross's theory r_2 is a function of T but not t. But this substantive assumption is hidden behind an ambiguous notation. In the present notation Cross's variable r_2 would be written as $E_1(T)\{\dot{q}_2(t)\}$. The fact that this depends on both T and t in general would then be apparent, and an equation of the form:

$$(1.1) \qquad E_1(T)\{\dot{q}_2(t)\} = r_2(T)$$

would display the assumption which is being made.

By developing a notation along these lines we may hope to isolate the many possible forms of dependence within a model and thence explore any new possibilities which are brought to light by the more developed notation. In this way we may facilitate generalisations of existing theories.

2. UTILITY MAXIMISATION

We are now in a position to set up a model of a bargainer's decision-making based on the principle of utility maximisation. First, we set out the assumptions on which the model will be based. The expectations of each bargainer regarding the other bargainer's behaviour is given by:

$$(1.2) \qquad E_i(T)\{q_j(t)\} = F_i\{t, q_i(T), q_j(T)\} \quad \begin{matrix} i = 1,2 \\ j = 1,2. \\ i \neq j \end{matrix}$$

18

The expectation of each bargainer regarding his own future behaviour is given by:

(1.3) $$E_i(T)\{q_i(t)\} = G_i\{t, q_i(T), q_j(T)\} \quad \begin{matrix} i = 1,2 \\ j = 1,2. \\ i \neq j \end{matrix}$$

It follows from these equations that bargainer i expects agreement to occur at that future time $t = t_i^*$ which is given by:

(1.4) $$E_i(T)\{q_j(t)\} + E_i(T)\{q_i(t)\} = M \quad \begin{matrix} i = 1,2 \\ j = 1,2. \\ i \neq j \end{matrix}$$

Furthermore, at time T, bargainer i expects to obtain agreement at the outcome $q_i = q_i^*$ which is given by:

(1.5) $$E_i(T)\{q_i^*\} = G_i\{t_i^*, q_i(T), q_j(T)\} \quad \begin{matrix} i = 1,2 \\ j = 1,2. \\ i \neq j \end{matrix}$$

Thus, at any present time T, bargainer i expects the eventual outcome q_i^* at a time t_i^* in the future.

We now set up the utility functions,

(1.6) $$u_i = u_i(q_i^*, t_i^*) \qquad i = 1,2.$$

Thus, to introduce the idea of utility maximising behaviour, we suppose that at every instant, T, bargainer i makes that demand which satisfies

(1.7) $$\frac{du_i}{dq_i} = 0$$

$$\frac{d^2u_i}{dq_i^2} < 0 \qquad i = 1,2$$

In setting up the utility functions (1.6), we have supposed that the utility of an expected outcome to a bargainer depends only on the expected outcome and on the future time at which it is expected. Forms of dependence other than this could quite plausibly be introduced, as Cross has shown.[1] The important point, however, is

---

[1] J. G. Cross, 'A Theory of the Bargaining Process,' Ph.D. thesis, Princeton University, Princeton, 1964, pp. 30–1, 92–92d.

19

to introduce a dependence of utility on the future time of agreement, for this is the factor underlying the whole dynamics of the bargaining process. As Cross puts it, 'If it did not matter when people agreed, it would not matter whether or not they agreed at all.'[1]

Examining equations (1.2) to (1.7), it becomes apparent that t_i^* and q_i^* are each functions of T. That is to say, the expected outcome and the expected time of agreement will in general change with time. This is the mechanism which underlies the workings of the model. We have not yet, however, developed enough ideas to discuss how these quantities will change over time. This is the topic to which we now turn.

3. DYNAMICS

The theoretical framework as we have developed it so far is still incomplete. This arises because in general the bargainers' expectations will not be fulfilled. Hence, to complete the picture, a theory of the adjustment of expectations is needed. The concern in this work, however, will be far more with the theory of decision-making based on changeable expectations than with the theory of the adjustment of these expectations. The following considerations of the adjustment process are therefore included for the sake of the completeness of the framework, and will have no real influence on the main argument of the work.

In order that the function which represents the expectations may change with experience, we must incorporate a new variable into the function. Thus, we now write

$$(1.8) \qquad E_t(T)\{q_j(t)\} = F_i\{t, q_i(T), q_j(T), V_{ij}(T)\} \qquad \begin{matrix} i = 1,2 \\ j = 1,2 \\ i \neq j \end{matrix}$$

where $V_{ij}(T)$ is a new adjustment variable. It is given the subscript ij because it refers to i's expectations of j's future behaviour. Unlike Cross's variable r_j, which represents i's expectation of j's concession rate, this variable V_{ij} does not have an immediate interpretation of this kind. It is a variable which serves to determine, graphically speaking, the actual position of expectations of a given form,

[1] J. G. Cross, 'A Theory of the Bargaining Process,' *American Economic Review*, 55, 1965, p. 72.

throughout future time. Suppose, for example, that i's expectations of j's future demands has the form shown as AB in Figure 1.5. This would arise, for example, from the assumption

$$(1.9) \qquad E_i(T)\{q_j(t)\} = \frac{V_{ij}}{t + V_{ij}} \, q_j(T).$$

Then, a change in V_{ij} from V'_{ij} to V''_{ij} results in the expectations curve shifting from AB to AC, say.

We may distinguish between the 'form' and the 'level' of expectations. By the form of expectations is meant the shape of the graph of $E_i(T)\{q_j(t))\}$ against t. This shape is fixed by the assumptions of the theory of expectations. By the level of expectations is meant the

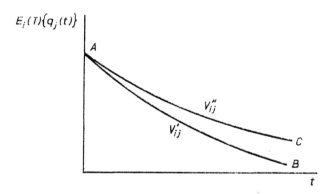

Fig. 1.5

height of this curve above the t-axis. This is determined by the value of V_{ij}. Thus, in the theory of expectations, V_{ij} serves to determine the level of expectations of a given form. We do not, at this stage, commit ourselves to any particular form of the expectations.

Within this notation, Cross's assumption would be

$$(1.10) \qquad E_i(T)\{q_j(t)\} = q_j(T) - V_{ij}t$$

so that here V_{ij} becomes identical with i's expectation of j's concession rate. This variable (Cross's r_j) determines the level of expectations which are always of a linear form.

If we suppose that the value of V_{ij} is responsive to i's experience of j's behaviour, then we can incorporate this variable into a theory of the adjustment of expectations. Such a theory is then reduced to a theory of the adjustment of the value of V_{ij}. A mechanism for this adjustment must now be adopted and the one we propose is a generalisation of that which is present in Cross's theory.[1] Very roughly, it depends on the comparison of expected with actual concession rates.

The concession rate of bargainer j as expected by bargainer i (i.e. the rate at which i expects j to decrease his demand) in the immediate future is simply minus the derivative with respect to t of $E_i(T)\{q_j(t)\}$ at $t = 0$. Thus,

$$\text{Expected concession rate} = -\frac{d}{dt} F_i\{t, q_i(T), q_j(T), V_{ij}(T)\} \text{ at } t = 0.$$

On the other hand, the actual concession rate of bargainer j at any point in time is simply minus the derivative with respect to T of the actual demand. Thus,

$$\text{Actual concession rate} = -\frac{dq_j}{dT}.$$

The theory of the adjustment process is now embodied in the following assumptions: (1) if the actual concession rate is equal to the expected concession rate, then V_{ij} remains constant and consequently the expectations remain unaltered;

(2) if the actual concession rate is different from the expected rate, then V_{ij} changes and the level of expectations changes;

(3) the adjustment variable V_{ij} changes at a rate which depends on the discrepancy or error between the expected and actual concession rates and in a direction which tends to eliminate this error.

If we make a simple linear assumption about the dependence of the variation of the adjustment variable with the error in the expected concession rate, we have the following theory of the adjustment of expectations:

$$(1.11) \qquad \frac{dV_{ij}}{dT} = \gamma_i \left[-\frac{d}{dt} F_i\{t, q_i, q_j, V_{ij}\}_{t=0} + \frac{dq_j}{dT} \right] \quad \begin{array}{l} i = 1,2 \\ j = 1,2. \\ i \neq j \end{array}$$

Here γ_i is an adjustment parameter which provides a measure of how sensitively bargainer i's expectations react to errors. We notice, in particular, that equation (1.11) is quite independent of the variable t

[1] *Ibid.* pp. 74–5.

and therefore deals exclusively with actual, as opposed to expected, changes. It can be seen that, although the adjustments are based on experience at the present moment ($t = 0$), the adjustment of V_{ij} affects expectations which extend into the future and, in this way, brings about changes in the expected agreement (q_i^*, t_i^*).

This now completes the description of the theoretical framework in mathematical form. We shall return to this framework in Chapter III and examine it in much greater detail in Chapter VI. In the meantime there is a digression on some existing theories of the bargaining process.

Chapter II

A BRIEF SURVEY OF BARGAINING THEORY

1. INTRODUCTION

In discussing theories of bargaining it is useful to make explicit the purpose which one expects such theories to serve. Criticism of the theories then revolves around their ability to serve this purpose. The purpose can be conveniently expressed by a list of questions to which the theories may be expected to provide answers. The present position is embodied in the following list.[1]

(1) What agreement (if any) is likely to result from the bargaining?

(2) What are the factors which play an important part in determining, or influencing, the outcome of the process?

(3) Given the initial conditions, what will be the course of developments which leads either to an agreement or to a break-down of the negotiations?

(4) What distinguishes those conditions under which an agreement of some form is likely to occur from those under which a breakdown of the negotiations is likely?

(5) Supposing there is, in answer to question 1, an equilibrium outcome, under what conditions will this be stable and under what conditions unstable? We realise that there are a number of possible senses of stability.[2] Here we will consider stability in

---

[1] For an alternative list see G. L. S. Shackle, 'The Nature of the Bargaining Process,' in *The Theory of Wage Determination* edited by J. T. Dunlop, Macmillan, London, 1964, Chapter 19.

[2] See P. A. Samuelson, *Foundations of Economic Analysis*, Harvard University Press, Cambridge, Mass., 1961, Chapter IX.

the following sense: an equilibrium outcome $\bar{f}$ is stable if the solution $f(T)$ satisfies the condition

$$(2.1) \qquad\qquad \operatorname*{Lim.}_{T \to \infty} f(T) = \bar{f}$$

irrespective of the initial conditions. This is what Samuelson calls 'perfect stability of the first kind'.[1]

The existing theories of bargaining will now be considered in relation to these questions. It will become quite manifest that most writers have been interested in finding answers to questions 1 and 2. Little concern has been shown in the search for answers to questions 3, 4 and 5. (Cross is the notable exception here, as will be seen.)

2. EXISTING THEORIES

How do existing theories explain the very general phenomena associated with the bargaining process? We shall review this question by starting with theories involving the smallest number

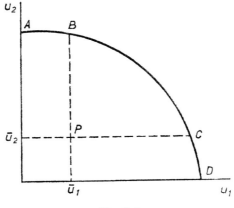

Fig. 2.1

of variables and adding, as we proceed, new variables which represent further factors assumed to affect the workings of the process.

[1] *Ibid.* p. 261.

25

Suppose we have two utility functions u_1 and u_2 upon which is imposed a constraint expressed by the welfare frontier $g(u_1, u_2) = 0$. There is also a point of disagreement, $\bar{u}_1$, $\bar{u}_2$, which we suppose lies below and to the left of the welfare frontier. This is shown in Figure 2.1. The two individuals may experience any pair of utilities below and to the left of the welfare frontier AD but if they cannot agree on the point at which to settle they will experience the pair $\bar{u}_1$, $\bar{u}_2$. We shall now proceed to review a number of theories which have been developed within this framework.

A. Edgeworth

Edgeworth's theory,[1] thus formulated, would give as a solution the entire section of the welfare frontier BC for which $u_1 > \bar{u}_1$, $u_2 > \bar{u}_2$. This is the classical conclusion that the outcome is indeterminate within some range (and we are merely taking Edgeworth as representative of those economists who have announced the indeterminacy of bilateral monopoly). Such a conclusion amounts to the assertion that questions 1, 2 and 3 above are unanswerable, a conclusion which in any case would seem compelling in the absence of a considerably enriched theoretical framework. Coming to question 4, the observation that agreement is sometimes not reached would have to be explained, within this framework, by saying that the disagreement point, P, lies above and to the right of $ABCD$. (Strictly, P would then be a part of the welfare frontier even though it is not joined to the remaining parts.) In Edgeworth's terms this would amount to saying that there is no contract zone, or no mutually advantageous adjustments which can be made from the disagreement point. Thus the theory is testable in the following way. If a situation exists in which there are mutually advantageous bargains for the two individuals, and yet disagreement

---

[1] F. Y. Edgeworth, *Mathematical Psychics*, C. Kegan Paul, London, 1881, pp. 20–30.

ensues, then the Edgeworth theory cannot be regarded as giving a satisfactory answer to question 4.

The question of stability (question 5, above) raises some problems since stability is a property which qualifies equilibria. And it is debatable whether an infinite set of points (*BC*) can properly be referred to as an equilibrium. However, it does seem to make sense to raise the question of stability in the following way: does the process eventually lead to an outcome somewhere along *BC* irrespective of the initial conditions? It may be noted that one cannot answer any questions regarding stability in the absence of a theory of the dynamics of the process, however fragmentary this theory may be. Edgeworth argues that whenever the individuals are below and to the left of *BC* there will be mutually advantageous trading bringing them closer to *BC*. Thus he writes '. . . that the joint-team should never be urged in a direction contrary to the *preference* of either individual; that the resultant line of force (and the momentum) of the . . . system should be continually intermediate between the (positive directions of the) lines of the respective pleasure-forces'.[1] Edgeworth goes on to show that this leads to an outcome on the contract curve, or, within the present framework, on *BC*, and we may conclude that he regarded the outcome as stable in the above sense.

B. *von Neumann and Morgenstern*

These writers have arrived at essentially the same conclusion as Edgeworth regarding the outcome of the process.[2] However, their mode of analysis was quite different, the situation being represented by a two-person non-zero-sum game, arising as the two-person case of the 'general game'.[3] Von Neumann and Morgenstern describe their solution as follows:[4] 'It consists of

[1] *Ibid.* p. 24.
[2] J. von Neumann and O. Morgenstern, *Theory of Games and Economic Behavior*, J. Wiley & Sons, New York, 1964, pp. 555–7.
[3] *Ibid.* pp. 504–5.
[4] *Ibid.* p. 555.

all those imputations where each player gets individually at least that amount which he can secure for himself, while the two get together precisely the maximum amount which they can secure together.' Since von Neumann and Morgenstern create a system in which interpersonal comparisons of utilities are legitimate, the maximum amount which the players can secure together is a meaningful concept within their special system. They write:

'We wish to concentrate on one problem—which is not that of the measurement of utilities and of preferences—and we shall therefore attempt to simplify all other characteristics as far as reasonably possible. We shall therefore assume that the aim of all participants in the economic system, consumers as well as entrepreneurs, is money, or equivalently a single monetary commodity. This is supposed to be unrestrictedly divisible and substitutable, freely transferable and identical, even in the quantitative sense, with whatever satisfaction or "utility" is desired by each participant.'[1]

If one does not make such assumptions, then $u_1 + u_2$ has no significance and one obviously cannot talk about its maximum value.

It can be seen that the von Neumann and Morgenstern theory of non-zero-sum games still leaves the outcome determined only up to any side payment which leaves each player with at least the amount he could have secured for himself, irrespective of his opponent's actions. But in a bargaining situation the amount which a player can guarantee for himself irrespective of his opponent's actions is just the utility of disagreement. It follows that the von Neumann and Morgenstern theory arrives at the same conclusion as Edgeworth. The remarks we have made regarding the Edgeworth solution therefore apply again to this case, *mutatis mutandis*.

[1] *Ibid.* p. 8.

We will be taking up the discussion of the game-theoretic approach to the bargaining process at a later point (Chapters IV and V).

C. Zeuthen

Zeuthen's theory[1] will be considered in the way it appears after Harsanyi's reformulation.[2] Harsanyi has shown that Zeuthen's theory predicts as the outcome of the process the u_1, u_2 which maximises $(u_1 - \bar{u}_1)(\bar{u}_2 - u_2)$. Except with rather pathological welfare frontiers this will be a unique outcome, as we shall see. This provides answers to questions 1 and 2 above.

In order to see how this conclusion arises, and how the remaining questions are answered, we must give a brief resumé of the substance of Zeuthen's theory. This will be done in terms of Harsanyi's reformulation.

Suppose that the utility of the outcome for bargainer i as demanded by bargainer j is u_{ij}. Then, it would be rational for bargainer 1, say, to take any risk of disagreement r_1 where

$$(2.2) \qquad (1 - r_1)u_{11} + r_1\bar{u}_1 \geqslant u_{12}.$$

Similarly, bargainer 2 would take any risk of disagreement r_2 where

$$(2.3) \qquad (1 - r_2)u_{22} + r_2\bar{u}_2 \geqslant u_{21}.$$

Rearranging these we have

$$(2.4) \qquad r_1 \geqslant \frac{u_{11} - u_{12}}{u_{11} - \bar{u}_1}.$$

$$(2.5) \qquad r_2 \geqslant \frac{u_{22} - u_{21}}{u_{22} - \bar{u}_2}.$$

Zeuthen then makes the assumption that the bargainer who can

[1] F. Zeuthen, *Problems of Monopoly and Economic Warfare*, Routledge & Sons, London, 1930, pp. 104–50.
[2] J. C. Harsanyi, 'Approaches to the Bargaining Problem before and after the Theory of Games,' *Econometrica*, 24, 1956, pp. 144–57.

afford the least risk of disagreement is the one to make a concession i.e. 1 makes a concession if

(2.6)
$$\frac{u_{11} - u_{12}}{u_{11} - \bar{u}_1} < \frac{u_{22} - u_{21}}{u_{22} - \bar{u}_2}.$$

It will be convenient if we transform the coordinates u_1, u_2 so that the point of disagreement is at the origin, i.e. we set $\bar{u}_1 = 0$, $\bar{u}_2 = 0$. It will be remembered that even the strongest measure of utility is determined only up to any positive linear transformation, so that such an adjustment of the utility functions is quite in order. In the new system of coordinates, the condition (2.6) becomes

$$\frac{u_{11} - u_{12}}{u_{11}} < \frac{u_{22} - u_{21}}{u_{22}}$$

or, rearranging this,

(2.7)
$$u_{11}u_{21} < u_{12}u_{22}.$$

Thus, according to Zeuthen's theory, 1 makes a concession if the condition (2.7) holds and 2 makes one if the inequality is reversed. Each one must clearly keep conceding until the inequality is reversed, in which case it becomes the other bargainer's turn to concede. Since $u_{11}u_{21}$ is the value of u_1u_2 as demanded by 1 and $u_{12}u_{22}$ is the value of u_1u_2 as demanded by 2, such a procedure will, under suitable conditions, lead to an agreement where u_1u_2 has its maximum value. (More will be said about these 'suitable conditions'.) It is not proposed to enter here into a discussion of the plausibility of these assumptions. This has been done quite thoroughly elsewhere.[1] Rather,

[1] See R. L. Bishop, 'A Zeuthen-Hicks Theory of Bargaining,' *Econometrica*, 32, 1964, pp. 410–17; J. G. Cross, 'A Theory of the Bargaining Process,' Ph.D. thesis, Princeton University, Princeton, 1964, pp. 10–16; J. Pen, *The Wage Rate under Collective Bargaining*, Harvard University Press, Cambridge, Mass., 1959, pp. 117–27; E. Saraydar, 'Zeuthen's Theory of Bargaining; A Note,' *Econometrica*, 33, 1965, pp. 802–5; G. L. S. Shackle, 'The Nature of the Bargaining Process,' in *The Theory of Wage Determination* edited by J. T. Dunlop, Macmillan, London, 1964, pp. 292–314.

we are concerned at the present with their explanatory power.

Suppose we begin with a situation as shown in Figure 2.2. The point of disagreement is at the origin and the welfare frontier can be written equivalently as $u_1 = g_1(u_2)$ or $u_2 = g_2(u_1)$. Initially, 1 is demanding an agreement at P_1 and 2 is demanding an agreement at P_2. Now, if a concession by 1

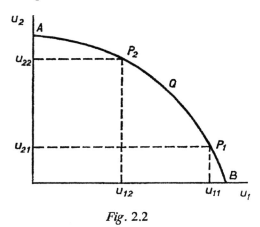

Fig. 2.2

moving along the welfare frontier results in an increase in $u_{11}u_{21}$, and if a concession by 2 moving along the welfare frontier results in an increase in $u_{12}u_{22}$, then the process converges to some point Q where u_1u_2 is a maximum along the welfare frontier. The conditions for this to happen are:

$$\frac{d}{du_1}(u_1u_2) < 0$$

(2.8)   i.e. $u_1g_2'(u_1) + g_2(u_1) < 0$ along P_1Q,

$$\frac{d}{du_2}(u_1,u_2) < 0$$

(2.9)   i.e. $u_2g_1'(u_2) + g_1(u_2) < 0$ along P_2Q,

i.e. $\dfrac{du_2}{du_1} + \dfrac{u_2}{u_1} < 0$ along P_1Q, from (2.8)

> 0 along P_2Q, from (2.9).

31

Also, the condition for u_1u_2 to be a maximum at Q is

$$\frac{d}{du_1}(u_1u_2) = \frac{d}{du_2}(u_1u_2) = 0,$$

(2.10) i.e. at $Q, \dfrac{du_2}{du_1} + \dfrac{u_2}{u_1} = 0,$

consistent with (2.8) and (2.9).
The condition is therefore

(2.11) $\dfrac{du_2}{du_1} + \dfrac{u_2}{u_1} \begin{array}{l} < 0 \text{ along } P_1Q \\ = 0 \text{ at } Q \\ > 0 \text{ along } P_2Q. \end{array}$

We can now illustrate how a situation might arise in which this process does not lead to an agreement.

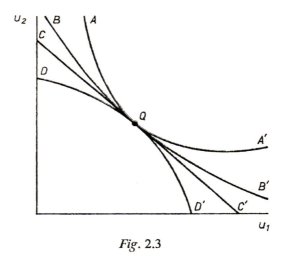

Fig. 2.3

Figure 2.3 shows a number of possible welfare frontiers. All the curves pass through a common point Q, and all of them are asumed to satisfy $\dfrac{d}{du_1}(u_1u_2) = \dfrac{d}{du_2}(u_1u_2) = 0$ at that point. BB' is the rectangular hyperbola $u_1u_2 = k$. For BB' the condition $\dfrac{du_2}{du_1} + \dfrac{u_2}{u_1} = 0$ is satisfied everywhere along the curve.

32

Now consider any curve which is more convex to the origin than BB' e.g. AA'. Along the portion $A'Q$, for any given u_1, u_2 and $\dfrac{du_2}{du_1}$ will be greater than the corresponding values along BB' and hence the condition (2.8) is not satisfied along $A'Q$. Similarly the condition (2.9) is not satisfied along AQ either. Hence, any curve more convex than BB' will not satisfy the condition (2.11) and concessions by either bargainer will not increase the product u_1u_2 along the curve but rather decrease it. The point Q on AA' in fact represents a minimum value of

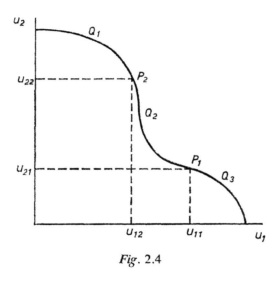

Fig. 2.4

u_1u_2. Thus with a welfare frontier like AA' agreement would not occur, according to Zeuthen's theory. This answers question 4, above. Note that the frontier BB' has the property that, even within Zeuthen's theory, the outcome is indeterminate within the range $u_1 > 0$, $u_2 > 0$. This is because u_1u_2 is constant along the curve and hence takes its maximum value at every point.

In the case of a welfare frontier like AA', disagreement occurs because no solution (i.e. no maximum value of u_1u_2) exists. This is not the only explanation of disagreement which is possible within the framework of Zeuthen's theory. Also, we

33

could have disagreement resulting from the existence of multiple solutions. This is illustrated in Figure 2.4 where Q_1, Q_3 are (local) maxima and Q_2 is a minimum value of u_1u_2. Since u_1u_2 increases from Q_2 to Q_1 and from Q_2 to Q_3, we see that if the initial demands are at opposite sides of Q_2, as shown, then the process does not converge.

We now turn to question 5, the question of stability. It follows from the above analysis that if a solution exists it will

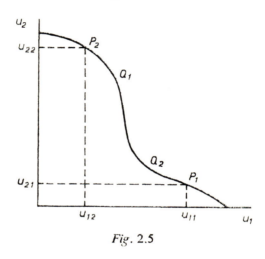

Fig. 2.5

possess stability in the small. That is, the solution will be stable if the initial demands of the bargainers are sufficiently close to the solution. To guarantee stability in the large it would be necessary not only for the maximum of u_1u_2 to be unique, but also for there to be no minima of u_1u_2. That this should be so is illustrated by a situation in which a unique maximum and a minimum along the welfare frontier exist in a situation which would not converge to an agreement. This is shown in Figure 2.5, where Q_1 is a maximum of u_1u_2 and Q_2 a minimum. It can be seen that with initial demands like P_1 and P_2 the process will fail to converge. Of course, with a welfare frontier which is everywhere concave to the origin, no divergence or instability can occur.

34

Thus, concluding our discussion of Zeuthen's theory, we see that however naive and implausible its behaviour assumptions, it does at least provide some answers to the questions listed at the beginning of this chapter.

D. Nash

Here, attention will be directed to Nash's first, 'fixed threat'[1] theory.[2] As Harsanyi has shown[3] Nash's theory predicts an outcome which is identical with that predicted by Zeuthen. However, the interesting thing is that the two theories rest on quite different reasoning. Whereas Zeuthen's rests on a theory of individual decision-making regarding concession-making behaviour, Nash's rests on a set of conditions which, it is supposed, the *joint* outcome must satisfy.[4] For this reason it is hardly surprising that Nash's theory has appeared to many writers more like something out of welfare economics.[5] Nevertheless, it should be pointed out that we are taking a positive interpretation of the theory here.

The axioms which Nash postulates to be satisfied by the joint outcome of the process are as follows:

(1) It is independent with respect to utility transformations. This assumption means that the solution must be independent of the units and origins of the utility functions.

---

[1] See p. 7.

[2] J. F. Nash, 'The Bargaining Problem,' *Econometrica*, 18, 1950, pp. 155–62.

[3] Harsanyi, *loc. cit.*

[4] In a later paper, (J. F. Nash, 'Two-person Cooperative Games,' *Econometrica*, 21, 1953, pp. 128–40), Nash complements this axiomatic approach with some reasoning involving a two-stage non-cooperative game model.

[5] See R. L. Bishop, 'Game-theoretic Analyses of Bargaining,' *Quarterly Journal of Economics*, 77, 1963, pp. 559–602; R. D. Luce and H. Raiffa, *Games and Decisions*, J. Wiley & Sons, New York, 1957, pp. 124–34; M. Shubik, *Strategy and Market Structure*, J. Wiley & Sons, New York, 1959, pp. 48–51; who all take a normative interpretation of the Nash solution.

(2) It is Pareto optimal.

(3) It is independent of irrelevant alternatives. This assumption means that if new outcome possibilities are added to a bargaining situation in such a way that the disagreement point remains unchanged, either the solution is unchanged or the solution appears among the new outcome possibilities.

(4) It reflects the symmetry of the formalisation. This assumption means that if a formalisation of the situation puts the bargainers into completely symmetrical positions, the solution must give them equal utility payoffs within that formalisation.

Nash has shown[1] that the only solution which satisfies these axioms is the solution (u_1, u_2) which maximises $(u_1 - \bar{u}_1)$ $(u_2 - \bar{u}_2)$. By the very nature of his argument Nash has nothing to say about the process by which an agreement is reached. Thus, although the theory provides answers to questions 1 and 2, the questions 3, 4 and 5 concerning the course of developments, how disagreement can occur and the stability of the outcome, are not really illuminated by Nash's contribution. (This criticism would, of course, be inappropriate if one took a normative interpretation of the theory.) It could be said in answer to 4, that disagreement would occur if $u_1 u_2$ has no maximum or multiple turning values with the initial demands insufficiently close to a maximum, but Nash rules out this possibility by assuming that the welfare frontier encloses a region which is compact and convex. It is obvious if the case of multiple maxima were allowed, the problem of choosing among the multiple Nash solutions would raise the bargaining problem all over again.

Suppose now we introduce a further variable x, say, which represents the possible outcomes of the bargaining process. The utility functions u_1, u_2 will be functions of this variable and so we write $u_1 = u_1(x)$, $u_2 = u_2(x)$. The previous constraint expressed by a welfare frontier may now be obtained by the condition for agreement, that the value of x must be the same

[1] Nash, *loc. cit.*

in both functions when agreement occurs.[1] Thus, the welfare frontier arises by eliminating x between the two utility functions. With this slightly enlarged framework we may go on to consider further existing theories.

E. Pen

We give here a very brief outline of Pen's theory.[2] Pen supposes that each utility function displays a maximum at some value of x. Let us call these values x_1^m for bargainer 1 and x_2^m for bargainer 2. These are the most preferred outcomes for which each bargainer will presumably strive. Suppose now that the outcome under consideration is x. Then, in an attempt to secure the outcome x bargainer 1 will take any risk of disagreement r_1 such that

$$(2.12) \qquad (1 - r_1)[u_1(x_1^m) - u_1(x)] > r_1[u_1(x) - \bar{u}_1].$$

Thus, bargainer 1 will take any risk of disagreement up to

$$(2.13) \qquad r_1^m = \frac{u_1(x_1^m) - u_1(x)}{u_1(x_1^m) - \bar{u}_1}.$$

Bargainer 1 will therefore yield and accept the outcome x when the risk of disagreement reaches this level. Pen then introduces a 'risk valuation function', Φ_1, to allow for deviations from the 'acturial mentality'. The condition for 1 to accept the outcome x then becomes

$$(2.14) \qquad r_1^m = \Phi_1 \left[\frac{u_1(x_1^m) - u_1(x)}{u_1(x_1^m) - \bar{u}_1} \right].$$

---

[1] Note that this is a different convention from the one employed in Chapter I, where the condition for agreement (involving demands rather than outcomes) is $q_1 + q_2 = M$ rather than $q_1 = q_2$.

[2] J. Pen, 'A General Theory of Bargaining,' *American Economic Review*, 42, 1952, pp. 24–42.

Finally, Pen supposes that the risk of disagreement, as estimated by bargainer 1, depends on the 'net contract utility' of bargainer 2, $u_2(x) - \bar{u}_2$, i.e.,

$$(2.15) \qquad r_1 = \Psi_1[u_2(x) - \bar{u}_2].$$

Hence, according to Pen, bargainer 1 gives in when $r_1 > r_1^m$ and thus he is on the point of agreeing to the outcome x when

$$(2.16) \qquad \Psi_1[u_2(x) - \bar{u}_2] = \Phi_1 \left[\frac{u_1(x_1^m) - u_1(x)}{u_1(x_1^m) - \bar{u}_1} \right].$$

Similarly, 2 is on the point of agreeing to the outcome x when

$$(2.17) \qquad \Psi_2[u_1(x) - \bar{u}_1] = \Phi_2 \left[\frac{u_2(x_2^m) - u_2(x)}{u_2(x_2^m) - \bar{u}_2} \right].$$

Given the functions and parameters of the problem, each of these equations determines a particular value of x, the outcome variable. Pen points out that these two equations, (2.16) and (2.17), will in general determine inconsistent outcomes and he supposes that the bargaining process consists in producing such shifts in the functions and parameters of the problem as to render the two outcomes determined by (2.16) and (2.17) consistent with one another. But there is no indication in Pen's theory as to which shifts will take place, how they will be brought about or what outcome they will lead to. (Pen does hint at how some shifts might occur in his discussion of the theory, however.) Hence, the most important feature of Pen's theory is that it is indeterminate. One can admit that Pen's formalism gives some insight into the operation of uncertainty and risk-taking in bargaining situations and that he has some suggestive things to say about the nature of economic power. But Pen presents his work as 'A General Theory of Bargaining', and continually, throughout the article, makes claims to the generality of his theory. For example, Pen writes:

. . . can we . . . legitimately stick to our thesis that our equations determine the outcome of the bargaining? We can.

38

For the theory indicates the factors that determine the outcome. Although the equations do not primarily aim at quantitative goals, they make the result of the bargaining determinate, in the sense that they give a condensed theory of the determination of the result. . . . The determining factors are not only enumerated, but their interplay is also exposed.'[1]

For a theory which quite patently makes no attempt to predict the outcome of the process, these claims seem totally unjustified. I find Pen's argument here altogether mistaken. Pen could rightly have claimed to have outlined the elements for a theory of bargaining and his discussion of those factors which must be considered in building such a theory includes much that is illuminating. But his equations (2.16) and (2.17) do not determine a static equilibrium since, as Pen readily admits, they are in general inconsistent with one another; neither does the theory have anything to say about the dynamics of the process, i.e. about the shifts by which the two equations are rendered consistent with one another. Thus, whether or not Pen's work can properly be called a general theory of bargaining, it cannot properly be called a determinate theory either in a static or dynamic sense.

Strangely enough, Pen quite clearly saw exactly this fault in Shackle's theory when he wrote:

'In my opinion, the theory of Shackle is to be seen as a valuable theory of the bargaining *plans*. It offers, however, no answer to the important question as to which final price will result from the clash of the conflicting plans. Therefore it cannot be maintained that Shackle determines the outcome of the bargaining, and in this respect his theory remains unsatisfactory'.[2]

It seems, however, that Shackle was fully aware of the situation when he wrote:

'. . . if exchange does take place, the price, in an important sense, is determinate: it is conceptually knowable in advance,

[1] *Ibid.* p. 39.   [2] *Ibid.* p. 26.

if we are fully informed about the gambler-preference system of each bargainer, and the function according to which he will draw inferences from a given sequence of "asking prices" or "offered prices" announced by the other bargainer.'[1]

Shackle's theory in fact gives no account of the functions according to which such inferences are drawn, but it is clear from this quotation that he was fully aware of the components needed for a determinate theory. He does, however, reveal some inconsistency when he claims, '. . . the outcome is *conceptually determinate* without reference to anything except the two bargainers tastes and *expectations*.'[2] Shackle's theory is not discussed in this work because Shackle was concerned primarily with a much wider problem than the bargaining process, namely the problem of decision-making under uncertain expectations. For this reason discussion of his theory would raise many issues much wider than the ones we are trying to analyse.

We may sum up our discussion of Pen's theory in his own words by saying that it offers no answer to the important question as to which outcome will result from the clash of the conflicting plans. In this respect his theory remains unsatisfactory and in view of our analysis we see that it offers an answer only to question 2, regarding the determinants of the process.

Suppose now we introduce a further variable into the situation—future time, t. We recall from Chapter I that future time is measured from the present moment as zero, so that any positive t represents an instant which lies in the future. With this enlarged framework we may go on to consider further theories.

[1] G. L. S. Shackle, *Expectation in Economics*, Cambridge University Press, Cambridge, England, 1949, p. 108.
[2] Shackle, *loc. cit.*

F Foldes and Bishop

There seem to be good reasons for taking these two theories together. First, they make the same overall point, namely that by introducing a principle of compromise based on the structure of time preferences of the bargainers, one can achieve a static equilibrium theory of the bargaining process. The principle of compromise differs between the two theories, but this overall point remains the same. Second, they were published almost simultaneously (Foldes[1] in February, 1964, Bishop[2] in July, 1964).

Introducing future time into the proceedings, we may now write the utility functions as

(2.18) $$u_1 = u_1(x,t),$$

(2.19) $$u_2 = u_2(x,t)$$

so that the utilities depend not only on the agreed outcome but also on the future time at which the agreement takes place. Suppose bargainer 1 is demanding the outcome x_1 and bargainer 2 is demanding the outcome x_2. Foldes' argument can then be summarised as follows. Suppose that

(2.20)
$$\frac{\partial u_1}{\partial x} > 0, \quad \frac{\partial u_2}{\partial x} < 0$$

$$\frac{\partial u_1}{\partial t} < 0, \quad \frac{\partial u_2}{\partial t} < 0$$

and $x_1 > x_2$ (so that a bargaining situation exists) then, for some value of t, $t = t_1$, we will have

(2.21) $$u_1(x_1,t) = u_1(x_2,0).$$

Also, for some value of t, $t = t_2$, we will have

(2.22) $$u_2(x_2,t) = u_2(x_1,0).$$

In other words, 1 thinks it is worthwhile holding out for his

[1] L. Foldes, 'A Determinate Model of Bilateral Monopoly,' *Economica*, 122, 1964, pp. 117–31.

[2] R. L. Bishop, 'A Zeuthen-Hicks Theory of Bargaining,' *Econometrica*, 32, 1964, pp. 410–17.

own demand for anything up to a time t_1 rather than accepting 2's offer immediately. Similarly, 2 thinks it is worthwhile holding out for anything up to a time t_2 rather than accepting 1's offer immediately. This is illustrated in Figure 2.6 where AB is an indifference curve for bargainer 2 and CD is an indifference curve for bargainer 1.

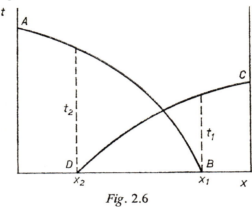

Fig. 2.6

Foldes' principle of compromise then consists of the following assumption: if $t_1 > t_2$, 1 can enforce his demand on 2; if $t_1 < t_2$, 2 can enforce his demand on 1; and if $t_1 = t_2$, the two demands are 'undecidable'. The equilibrium point is the point x_0 which is enforceable against all other points. Foldes' theory predicts that, abstracting from uncertainty, this outcome x_0 will be agreed upon immediately.

Recalling the notation used in discussing Zeuthen's theory, we may now outline the principle of Bishop's theory which he calls 'A Zeuthen-Hicks Theory of Bargaining', referring to its theoretical antecedents.

Utilities are now interpreted as signifying payoff per unit of time. Suppose the two bargainers discount future benefits at the instantaneously compounded rates a_1, a_2 respectively. (Notice that this is less general than Foldes' assumption that $\frac{\partial u_1}{\partial t} < 0$, $\frac{\partial u_2}{\partial t} < 0$.) Then, the present value to 1 of immediately conceding to 2's demand is

(2.23) $$\int_0^\infty u_{12}e^{-a_1 t}\, dt = \frac{u_{12}}{a_1}.$$

The present value to 1 of winning his own demand after a breakdown[1] which reduces his utility to zero[2] for a period s_1 is

(2.24) $$\int_{s_1}^\infty u_{11}e^{-a_1 t}\, dt = \frac{u_{11}}{a_1} e^{-a_1 s_1}.$$

Hence, under the optimistic expectation of complete victory after the breakdown, 1 can afford to tolerate a breakdown whose length is up to the s_1 which equates these two present values, i.e. which satisfies

$$\frac{u_{12}}{a_1} = \frac{u_{11}}{a_1} e^{-a_1 s_1}$$

(2.25) $$\text{i.e. } s_1 = \frac{\log u_{11} - \log u_{12}}{a_1}.$$

Similarly, under the same optimistic expectations, 2 can afford a breakdown whose length is up to

(2.26) $$s_2 = \frac{\log u_{22} - \log u_{21}}{a_2}.$$

Bishop's principle of compromise then consists of the assumption that the bargainer whose maximum tolerable length of breakdown is the smaller will make a concession. In other words, 1 makes a concession when $s_1 < s_2$, or, after some rearrangement, when

(2.27) $$u_{11}u_{21}^{(a_1/a_2)} < u_{12}u_{22}^{(a_1/a_2)}.$$

---

[1] Following Hicks and Zeuthen who were concerned with bargaining between unions and management, Bishop talks about a strike rather than a breakdown. Here, to preserve the generality of the discussion, we will speak of a breakdown of the bargaining.

[2] As with the discussion of Zeuthen's theory we again have the convention that the point of disagreement is at the origin.

Thus, the process is analogous to that described by Zeuthen's theory. Under suitable conditions concessions occur until the bargainers agree at the point where $u_1u_2{}^{(a_1/a_2)}$ is a maximum. In fact the solution is identical with Zeuthen's in the case where $a_1 = a_2$.

These theories provide answers to questions 1 and 2 concerning the outcome and the determinants of the process. Being derivative of Zeuthen's work, Bishop's theory also has something to say about the course of developments (question 3), although Foldes' theory being quite intentionally static, does not. The question whether agreement occurs or not would depend, with Foldes' theory, on the existence and uniqueness of an equilibrium point, and this Foldes discusses with considerable rigour.[1] In Bishop's theory the problems raised by this are analogous to those raised in Zeuthen's theory and making the appropriate substitutions of $u_1u_2{}^{(a_1/a_2)}$ for u_1u_2 our discussion of Zeuthen's theory applies equally well here. The question of stability does not arise in Foldes' static theory and in Bishop's it again gives rise to problems analogous to those discussed in connection with Zeuthen.

The theories of Bishop and Foldes are interesting in a number of ways. First, they contradict the traditional position that, as far as static equilibrium theory is concerned, the theory of bargaining is necessarily indeterminate.[2] Second, they contradict the views of Pen and Shackle that the determinacy of the process is to be found in the operation of uncertainty. Third, they stand in contrast to the more recent theory of Cross which, in the complete absence of an equilibrium theory

[1] Foldes, *op. cit.* pp. 125–30.

[2] Although Bishop considers the process by which concessions are made, it would be possible, and perhaps more natural, to present his theory in a static context by supposing that in the absence of uncertainty the bargainers agree to the outcome which maximises $u_1u_2{}^{a_1/a_2}$ immediately. As Bishop himself says of Zeuthen's theory (R. L. Bishop, 'A Zeuthen-Hicks Theory of Bargaining,' *Econometrica*, 32, 1964, p. 412) '. . . it really implies a fore-ordained outcome that the bargainers might just as well establish without any play-acting.' He regards this point as equally applicable to his own theory (*Ibid.* p. 417).

seeks the outcome in the dynamics of the process. It is to this development we now turn.

G. Cross

We will not present Cross's theory[1] here since this is done at some length in Chapter III where we show how it may be derived from the general framework presented in Chapter I. However, it does seem appropriate to point out here that Cross's theory has the following properties. There is no static equilibrium and hence the outcome can be anywhere in the contract zone. At the same time the theory is determinate, the actual outcome depending on the parameters of the situation and on the initial conditions. This, in effect, brings us back to something very much like Edgeworth's position. However, in the light of Cross's theory we would want to qualify and rephrase Edgeworth's position somewhat as follows. Although the outcome of the bargaining can be anywhere in the contract zone one can develop a theory which predicts the outcome of the process and this outcome depends on the initial conditions. Therefore, although this theory is indeterminate as far as static equilibrium constructions are concerned, the outcome is determinate within the dynamic model of the process.

Within the context of economic theory, this is an unusual situation methodologically. For it is customary to seek first a static equilibrium theory and then, having achieved this, to go on to develop a dynamic model to deal with the disequilibrium behaviour of a system. If we accept Cross's argument, then we can see why this kind of approach would be singularly disastrous in the case of the theory of bargaining. For an equilibrium outcome must be independent of the initial conditions of the system. So no amount of equilibrium analysis would ever have unearthed the Cross solution. Only by developing the dynamic

[1] J. G. Cross, 'A Theory of the Bargaining Process,' Ph.D. thesis, Princeton University, Princeton, 1964; J. G. Cross, 'A Theory of the Bargaining Process,' *American Economic Review*, 55, 1965, pp. 67–94.

model in the complete absence of any equilibrium theory can this solution be attained.

Since the Cross solution is not an equilibrium point, the question of stability does not arise, for stability is a property of equilibria. Although Cross's theory supplies answers to questions 1–4, question 5 cannot be properly addressed to it. There is, though, a similar and closely allied question. Whether agreement is reached or not depends on the covergence properties of the theory. Thus, we can say that agreement will be reached if, for some time, T,

(2.28) $$q_1(T) + q_2(T) \leqslant M.[1]$$

Substituting Cross's solution[2] (in the case of a linear learning model and linear utility functions $u_1(q_1) = \xi_1 q_1, u_2(q_2) = \xi_2 q_2$[3]) the condition for convergence becomes,

(2.29) $$\left[\frac{k_1}{a_1} + \frac{m_1}{a_2}\right]e^{w_1 T} + \left[\frac{k_2}{a_1} + \frac{m_2}{a_2}\right]e^{w_2 T} \leqslant M + \frac{C_1}{a_1 \xi_1} + \frac{C_2}{a_2 \xi_2},$$

where

$$w_1 = \frac{-\alpha_1 - \alpha_2 + \sigma}{2(1 - A_1 A_2)},$$

$$w_2 = \frac{-\alpha_1 - \alpha_2 - \sigma}{2(1 - A_1 A_2)},$$

$$\sigma = |[(\alpha_1 - \alpha_2)^2 + 4\alpha_1\alpha_2 A_1 A_2]^{\frac{1}{2}}|,$$

$$A_1 = \frac{\alpha_1}{a_1},$$

$$A_2 = \frac{\alpha_2}{a_2}.$$

[1] Here we are reverting to the original convention for the condition of agreement, as used in Chapter I.

[2] J. G. Cross, 'A Theory of the Bargaining Process,' Ph.D. thesis, Princeton University, Princeton, 1964, pp. 76–80.

[3] Some of Cross's symbols have been changed to bring them into line with the present notation.

46

k_1, k_2, m_1, m_2 are constants defined in terms of other parameters, C_1, C_2 are costs of bargaining per period, and α_1, α_2 are learning parameters defined in Chapter III.

Since the right-hand side of (2.29) is positive, it follows that a sufficient condition for (2.29) to be true for some T is that w_1, w_2 are both negative. In this case the equation will hold for sufficiently large T. With a little rearrangement w_1, w_2 can be written as

$$w_1 = \frac{-(\alpha_1 + \alpha_2) + |[(\alpha_1 + \alpha_2)^2 + 4\alpha_1\alpha_2(A_1A_2 - 1)]^{\frac{1}{2}}|}{2(1 - A_1A_2)}$$

(2.30)

$$w_2 = \frac{-(\alpha_1 + \alpha_2) - |[(\alpha_1 + \alpha_2)^2 + 4\alpha_1\alpha_2(A_1A_2 - 1)]^{\frac{1}{2}}|}{2(1 - A_1A_2)}$$

It can be seen that these will both be negative if $A_1A_2 < 1$. Thus a condition for convergence is $A_1A_2 < 1$, a sufficient condition for which is $A_1 < 1$, $A_2 < 1$ (since A_1, A_2 are both positive). Cross arrives at this condition by a rather different procedure[1] and, rather misleadingly, refers to it as a stability condition.[2] In terms of the original parameters of the model, the condition can be written

(2.31) $\qquad\qquad \alpha_1 < a_1; \alpha_2 < a_2.$

The significance of this result will now be pointed out. It implies that, even when a contract zone exists, the bargainers may or may not reach some agreement within the contract zone depending on the relationship between parameters representing their learning and discounting behaviour. This is

[1] J. G. Cross, 'A Theory of the Bargaining Process,' *American Economic Review*, 55, 1965, pp. 80–1.
[2] This could properly be called a stability condition in the sense that the ratio of the expected concession rates (r_1/r_2) has an equilibrium value in the theory even though q_1, q_2 do not. But to talk about stability in this connection seems to blur one's picture of the nature of Cross's solution in relation to other solutions where stability certainly refers to equilibrium values of q_1, q_2.

47

in complete contrast to the preceding theories which would have to explain the occurrence of disagreement by the absence of a contract zone (Edgeworth), the absence of an equilibrium point (Zeuthen, Nash, Foldes, Bishop) or the existence of inappropriate initial conditions relative to the equilibrium point (Zeuthen, Bishop).

Chapter III

CLOSED LOOPS

1. CROSS'S ASSUMPTIONS

The framework we have constructed in chapter I is much too general to have any significant implications regarding the workings of bargaining processes. In the present chapter we wish to consider sets of assumptions which are special cases of this framework. First we will consider the assumptions made by Cross.[1] These can be summarised as follows.

I. *Independence assumption.* It is assumed that each bargainer expects the other bargainer's future sequence of demands to be independent of his own current demand. This implies the attitude: 'What I do will not affect what you are going to do.' As Cross puts it, 'By restricting our simple model to bargaining situations in which bluffing does not occur, we have already assumed that player I does not think of r_2 [1's expectation of 2's rate of concession] as a function of his own behavior.'[2] Within our formalism this amounts to the assumption that $E_i(T)\{q_j(t)\}$ is independent of $q_i(T)$. This is obviously quite a strong assumption and amounts to the proposal to neglect one of the possible forms of interaction.

II. *Linearity assumption.* It is assumed that each bargainer has expectations of the other bargainer's demand which are linear

---

[1] J. G. Cross, 'A Theory of the Bargaining Process,' *American Economic Review*, 55, 1965, pp. 67–94. It should be noted, however, that Cross did not present his assumptions as a special case of this framework but, on the contrary, as a generalisation into dynamics of the theories which precede his own. [2] *Ibid.* p. 73.

in future time. In other words, each bargainer expects the other to concede at a constant rate.

III. *Pure intransigence assumption.* It is assumed that each bargainer plans to maintain his current demand until an agreement is reached. Each is expecting the other to make all the concessions.

With these three assumptions, equations (1.1) and (1.2) become

(3.1) $$E_i(T)\{q_j(t)\} = q_j(T) + V_{ij}(T)t,$$

(3.2) $$E_i(T)\{q_i(t)\} = q_i(T).$$

Then, using equation (1.11), it follows that the adjustment of expectations is represented by

(3.3) $$\frac{dV_{ij}}{dT} = \gamma_i\left[-V_{ij} + \frac{dq_j}{dT}\right].$$

Writing the expected concession rate $-V_{ij} = r_j$ then yields Cross's 'learning model'.[1] Interestingly enough, M. J. Bailey has, in a macroeconomic context, a theory of the adjustment of expectations which is formally identical with Cross's but expressed in difference rather than differential equations.[2] Bailey supposes[3] that, if the actual value of a variable in period k is X_k and its expected value in that period is X_k^*, we can write an equation of the form

$$X_{k+1}^* = \beta X_k + (1 - \beta)X_k^*$$

which leads, on rearrangement, to

$$X_{k+1}^* - X_k^* = \beta\{X_k - X_k^*\}$$

or

$$\Delta X_k^* = \beta\{X_k - X_k^*\},$$

---

[1] *Ibid.* p. 88.
[2] M. J. Bailey, *National Income and the Price Level*, McGraw-Hill, New York, 1962, Chapter IX.
[3] *Ibid.* p. 228.

i.e. the change in the expected value per period is proportional to the error in the expectations. Cross's theory involves just this assumption but by using differential equations it proceeds to the limiting case where the length of each period becomes vanishingly small.

IV. *Exponential discounting assumption.* It is assumed that the discounting function varies exponentially with future time. Strotz has shown[1] that this assumption is necessary if the model is to generate decisions at different points of time which are consistent with one another.

V. *Costs of bargaining assumption.* It is assumed that until agreement is reached there is a constant cost per period to the ith bargainer of C_i.

With these assumptions the utility function becomes[2]

$$(3.4) \qquad u_i = u_i(q_i)e^{-a_it_i^*} + \frac{C_i}{a_i}(e^{-a_it_i^*} - 1) \quad i = 1,2,$$

where $u_i(q)$ is the utility of the outcome q at the time of agreement and a_i is the discounting rate of bargainer i. Since q_i^* and t_i^* are given by equations (1.3) and (1.4), the utilities are now defined at any point of time and, by making use of the control he has over the variable q_i, the ith bargainer may engage in utility maximising behaviour. Under these assumptions (1.3) and (1.4) in fact take the form

$$(3.5) \qquad\qquad q_i^* = q_i(T),$$

$$(3.6) \qquad\qquad t_i^* = \frac{q_i(T) + q_j(T) - M}{r_j}.$$

Putting these expressions into (3.4) and setting $\dfrac{du_i}{dq_i} = 0$, we find

[1] R. H. Strotz, 'Myopia and Inconsistency in Dynamic Utility Maximization,' *Review of Economic Studies*, 23, 1956, pp. 165–80.
[2] Cross, *op. cit.* p. 74.

51

that a utility maximising bargainer will demand the q_i which satisfies

(3.7) $$\frac{a_i}{r_j}\left[u_i(q_i) + \frac{C_i}{a_i}\right] = u_i'(q_i).$$

(It is supposed throughout that the second order condition $\frac{d^2 u_i}{dq_i^2} < 0$ is satisfied.)

This concludes the brief review of the assumptions which are basic to Cross's theory. Although these assumptions may seem comparatively simple they give rise to a model which is rich in possibilities and which has implications that are neither trivial nor intuitively obvious.

2. REPRESENTATION OF THE MODEL

In order to see more clearly the structure of this model, we may employ the kind of diagrammatic representation used in the study of closed loop systems. At the same time, this may shed some light on the kind of structure to be expected of models within the decision/expectation/adjustment framework. To facilitate this we make two simplifying assumptions which are in no way essential to the workings of the model. First, we suppose that the utility functions are linear, $u_i(q_i) = \xi_i q_i$. Second, we neglect the fixed costs of bargaining by setting $C_i = 0$. The theory can then be represented by Figure 3.1. Here the variables are shown enclosed in circles and the relations between the variables are shown along the arrows connecting the circles. The determination of each variable can be understood by considering all the arrows which end on that variable. The variable at the beginning of each arrow is acted upon by the operator along the arrow and the resulting expressions, when summed, may be put equal to the variable at the end of the arrows. In this way the equations of the model may be generated.

It is immediately apparent from the diagram that the theory exhibits an overall closed loop structure. Each of the eight variables experiences feedback. There are also two subloops involving r_1, $\dot{r}_1$ and r_2, $\dot{r}_2$ respectively, corresponding to the

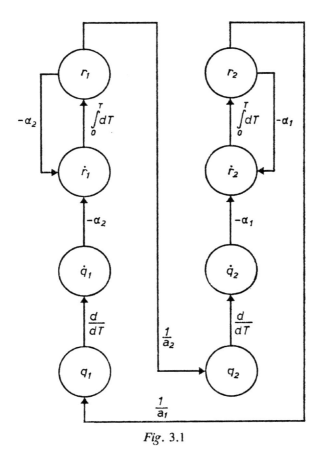

Fig. 3.1

feedback within the adjustment processes of each bargainer. Because of the overall loop structure, a change in any one variable has an effect which travels round the whole loop eventually affecting the original variable itself. Therefore, within the model as a whole, there is no one-way causation.

53

3. CLOSED LOOP MODELS

The theory of closed loop systems has been applied to macroeconomic problems by a number of writers.[1] If it is realised that self-steering mechanisms are an application of the theory of closed loop control systems, then it becomes apparent that this line of thought has also been taken up in political science[2] and the theory of international relations.[3] However, it is interesting to note that, as far as the author knows, the relevance of such models to the theory of microeconomic decision-making with more than one actor has not been discussed. Although this was not mentioned by Cross, his theory can be regarded formally as an application of such models to microeconomic theory. However, as will be seen, there is a significant theoretical difference between the applications of these ideas to macroeconomic and microeconomic theory.

In macroeconomics, the problems of stabilisation policy involve decisions to add a further closed loop to an existing model of the economy. The aim is to build into the system such negative feedback as will control the value of some variable. Usually the control consists of maintaining this variable close to some 'desirable' level. The variable which is controlled in this way is said to have been stabilised.[4] The

[1] A. W. Phillips, 'Stabilisation Policy in a Closed Economy,' *Economic Journal*, 64, 1954, pp. 290–323; A. Tustin, *The Mechanism of Economic Systems*, Heinemann, London, 1953; R. G. D. Allen, *Mathematical Economics*, Macmillan, London, 1959, Chapter 9.

[2] See K. W. Deutsch, *The Nerves of Government*, Free Press of Glencoe, New York, 1963. For example, Deutsch writes (*Ibid.* p. *ix*), 'This book suggests that it might be profitable to look upon government somewhat less as a problem of power and somewhat more as a problem of steering . .'.

[3] J. W. Burton, *International Relations: A General Theory*, Cambridge University Press, Cambridge, England, 1965, notably Chapter 12. Burton writes (*Ibid.* p. 2), '. . . to understand these aspects of relations between States, concepts, systems and models are required which relate to steering, to communication, to feed-back and to other aspects of decision-making.'

[4] Different forms of feedback may involve inputs which are proportional to the error between the relevant variable and its desired value, or the time

important point is that the original model of the economy can be assumed to respond passively to the addition of a closed loop. Whereas the workings of the stabilisation policy can be interpreted as a stream of error-actuated decisions intended to control a certain variable in the rest of the economy, the workings of the original closed loop system (the model of the economy without a stabilisation policy operating) cannot be interpreted as intended to control anything at all. No overall purpose can be assigned to the behaviour of the model since it consists of the aggregate effect of a great many independent decisions. So a reasonable, if somewhat crude, analogy to the stabilisation process is a single self-steering mechanism or servomechanism. A very different situation is found in the bargaining process in microeconomics. Here each bargainer is making error-actuated decisions but each is attempting to steer in a contrary way. An appropriate mechanical analogy for this situation might be a pair of linked servomechanisms, the output of each one being the input of the other. The outcome of such a situation would be expected to be quite sensitive to the relative performance of the two servomechanisms, and it is not immediately apparent whether either one's attempt at steering would be particularly successful.

In the light of these analogies we may return to comment further on the work of the above-mentioned writers who have each attempted to introduce the idea of self-steering mechanisms or communication and control models into various branches of the social sciences. For it is quite apparent from these contributions that the kind of model that these writers have in mind is one with a single self-steering mechanism operating in a relatively unsophisticated environment rather than a self-steering mechanism operating on (and being operated upon by) another

---

integral or the time derivative of this error or, more generally, linear combinations of all three kinds of feedback. These different forms of feedback have different properties as stabilising factors. For a more detailed discussion of these properties see Phillips, *loc. cit.*

such mechanism.[1] This situation is understandable when one considers the various contexts within which the models have been proposed. The functioning of domestic government may have structural similarities with a single self-steering mechanism in a fairly passive environment and the activities of the nation state in international politics may also take on this form when the nation is faced with a large number of small nations. It has already been argued, too, that this is the more appropriate model for the purposes of macroeconomic theory. It transpires, then, that within the social science context the concept of self-steering mechanisms have only been introduced and investigated in the limiting case where the environment may be regarded as essentially passive. This is not to say that the possibility of autonomous acts within the environment has been altogether excluded.[2] Rather, by characterising an environment as essentially passive we mean that it is of a much lower order of purposiveness than the centre of control we are considering. Or, to put the matter differently, an environment may be considered to be essentially passive if, when viewed as a self-steering mechanism, it is of a much lower order of sophistication in its functioning than the centre of control under consideration.

It is quite obvious that the limiting case of a passive environment is by far the simplest to deal with theoretically. It has been investigated in great detail in the theory of servo-mechanisms where the engineering applications of the subject dictate a concern with control processes which are predictable and likely to succeed in controlling something. The simpler the environment the more successful the self-steering process is

[1] I have dealt briefly with this question elsewhere in a slightly different context. See A. Coddington, 'Game Theory, Bargaining Theory and Strategic Reasoning,' *Journal of Peace Research*, Vol. 4, No. 1, pp. 39–45. See especially pp. 43–4.

[2] Deutsch, whose treatment of these problems goes by far the deepest seems aware of this possibility. But even in Deutsch's work the question of the nature of the environment's behaviour remains always peripheral and it seems implicit that this question does not raise significant and central issues for the model. (Deutsch, *op. cit.*)

likely to be. The theory has therefore been developed with a view to dealing with these simple environments.[1]

We may refer again, as we did in Chapter I, to the theory of markets where the limiting case of many buyers and sellers is the simplest case to deal with theoretically, since each actor may regard himself as acting in an essentially passive environment. As with buyers and sellers, so with self-steering mechanisms. And just as the theoretical problems of duopoly, bilateral monopoly and oligopoly are far more troublesome than those of perfect competition, so the interaction of two, or a small number, of self-steering mechanisms is much more formidable than those of a self-steering mechanism in an essentially passive environment. As has been remarked earlier, the results of such small-group steering processes would very much depend on the relative sophistication of the functioning of the various control centres. To what extent any one of them would succeed in steering is by no means a trivial question.

In view of this discussion, Cross's theory may be seen as an attempt to develop a theory of the two-actor case of interacting self-steering systems. As such, his theory is relevant to a 'nearly symmetrical' situation. Each actor exhibits expectations and learning behaviour of the same form, although the actual parameter values may differ from one actor to the other. Viewed within this wider context, Cross's contribution emerges as a pioneering venture of considerable significance.

[1] Perhaps we should include environments which contain strongly autonomous but random events in the class of simple environments.

Chapter IV

THE RELATIONSHIP BETWEEN DECISION-MAKING AND EXPECTATIONS

1. INTRODUCTION

In this chapter we will be raising some issues relating to the internal consistency of a wide class of bargaining models. In the course of this discussion we will come to what appears to be a central theoretical problem in dealing with decision-making in an environment containing only one other decision-maker and the analysis will bring us to make the distinction between self-replacing and self-generating decision rules.

2. THE QUESTION OF CONSISTENCY

The question of the consistency of decision-making and expectations may conveniently be referred to as the Cournot problem since it arises most forcefully and perhaps in its best known form in Cournot's theory of duopoly.[1] In a theory of duopoly it is required to arrive at a decision rule for the output of each duopolist under the circumstances that the price of the product is a function of the joint output of the two duopolists. Each duopolist is supposed to strive for the maximum profit he can achieve.

Since the profit gained by each duopolist depends on the output decisions of both of them, each duopolist must make his

[1] A. Cournot, *Researches into the Mathematical Principles of the Theory of Wealth*, translated by N. T. Bacon, Macmillan, New York, 1897.

58

maximising decision in the light of his expectations of how the other duopolist will respond. Duopolist 1 must begin with an expectation of duopolist 2's decision rule and then proceed to derive a decision rule of his own, depending on this expectation. Suppose that 1 expects that 2 follows the decision rule: keep the output constant at its present value. This expectation would lead 1 to adopt the decision rule: maximise profit with respect to my own output, treating the other duopolist's output as a parameter. In his theory, Cournot was concerned to trace the consequences of both duopolists operating with this second rule. It is, however, revealing to carry the reasoning about the decision rules themselves somewhat further. The situation so far is that duopolist 1 has supposed that 2 follows a decision rule, *A*, and this supposition has led 1 to adopt a quite different decision rule, *B*. In the Cournot theory each duopolist expects the other to do what he himself is quite patently not going to do. Following this line of thought, however, duopolist 1 may now reason that, since duopolist 2 is in exactly the same circumstances as he is, there is nothing preventing 2 from also arriving at decision rule *B*. But if 2 has arrived at decision rule *B*, this rule is itself no good for duopolist 1, since it is only effective for guaranteeing profit maximisation when 2 follows decision rule *A*.

In this way, duopolist 1 may suppose that 2 has arrived at decision rule *B*. If this is so, 2 is maximising his own profit with respect to variations in his own output and his behaviour may be represented by a reaction function $y_2 = h(y_1)$; y_1, y_2 being the outputs of the duopolists. In adopting his decision rule, 1 must take this dependence into account. Suppose that 1's profit is given by

(4.1) $$\pi_1 = H(y_1, y_2).$$

Then, in arriving at his new decision rule, 1 maximises the function $H[y_1, h(y_1)]$ with respect to y_1. This may be referred to as decision rule *C*. Duopolist 1's quest for consistency between his decision-making and his expectations has led him only to a new form of inconsistency. The expectation of 1 that 2 can also adopt decision rule B has driven 1 to adopt a quite different decision rule, C. The situation in which each duopolist expects the other to follow rule B and therefore each himself follows rule C has been referred to as a 'Stackelberg disequilibrium'.[1] This would constitute a theory of one order higher than that of Cournot.

3. DECISION-MAKING AND EXPECTATIONS IN THEORIES OF BARGAINING

Exactly the same reasoning applies within the present framework, *mutatis mutandis*, to the case of two bargainers. The assumption by 1 that bargainer 2 will follow decision rule A will lead bargainer 1 to follow decision rule B which, in general, will be different from rule A. He may then expect that 2 has also arrived at rule B, and this, in general, will lead him to still another rule, C. There appears to be no limit in principle to the levels of complexity to which the decision rules may be taken.

In the light of this discussion, we are led to make a distinction between two types of decision rule. We will say that R is a self-generating decision rule if it satisfies the following condition: when bargainer 1 expects bargainer 2 to follow the rule R, this leads 1 also to adopt the rule R. The decision rule R will be termed self-replacing if it satisfies the following condition: when bargainer 1 expects bargainer 2 to follow the rule R, this leads 1 to adopt some rule different from R. It can now be shown that the theories considered in Chapter II rest on self-replacing decision rules.[2]

---

[1] See J. M. Henderson and R. E. Quandt, *Microeconomic Theory*, McGraw-Hill, New York, 1958, pp. 180–1.

[2] Since Edgeworth and von Neumann and Morgenstern leave the outcome of the bargaining process indeterminate, they do not consider actual decision rules. Also the present discussion does not apply to Nash, who is concerned with joint decision rules rather than individual ones.

In Zeuthen's theory[1] bargainer 1 expects that 2 is following the rule: hold out for my own demand with probability p and concede completely to 1's demand with probability $(1 - p)$. This expectation leads 1, however, to follow the rule: make that partial concession, if any, which is just sufficient to ensure $u_{11}u_{21} > u_{12}u_{22}$.

In Pen's theory[2] we have the situation that 1 expects 2 to follow the rule: hold out for my own demand with probability p and concede completely to 1's demand with probability $(1 - p)$. This leads 1 to follow the rule: accept the outcome x which satisfies equation (2.15). (In general, x is different from both 1's demand and 2's demand.)

In Foldes' theory[3] bargainer 1 expects that bargainer 2 follows the decision rule: give in to 1 if my delay time, t_2, is less than his delay time, t_1.[4] This, according to Foldes, leads the bargainers to adopt the joint decision rule: settle immediately for that point which is enforceable against all other points.[5]

In Bishop's theory[6] bargainer 1 expects that bargainer 2 follows the decision rule: offer 1 u_{12} but if he allows the bargaining to break down, make a complete concession to his demand u_{11} at the end of the breakdown period. This leads bargainer 1 to adopt the decision rule: make that partial concession, if any, which is just sufficient to ensure the inequality $u_{11}u_{21}^{(a_1/a_2)} > u_{12}u_{22}^{(a_1/a_2)}$.

In Cross's theory[7] bargainer 1 expects that bargainer 2 follows the decision rule: concede at the constant rate r_2 or,

[1] F. Zeuthen, *Problems of Monopoly and Economic Warfare*, Routledge & Sons, London, 1930, pp. 104–50.

[2] J. Pen, 'A General Theory of Bargaining,' *American Economic Review*, 42, 1952, pp. 24–42.

[3] L. Foldes, 'A Determinate Model of Bilateral Monopoly,' *Economica*, 122, 1964, pp. 117–31.

[4] See p. 42.

[5] See p. 42.

[6] R. L. Bishop, 'A Zeuthen-Hicks Theory of Bargaining,' *Econometrica*, 32, 1964, pp. 410–17.

[7] J. G. Cross, 'A Theory of the Bargaining Process,' *American Economic Review*, 55, 1965, pp. 67–94.

in other words, choose the demand $q_2 = q_2^0 - r_2 T$. This leads bargainer 1 to adopt the decision rule: choose the q_1 which satisfies the equation (3.7) with $i = 1$, $j = 2$, i.e. the q_1 which maximises the present value of the expected outcome.

It can now be seen how one can proceed to higher order theories. For example, consider Cross's theory. Let us refer to $q_2 = q_2^0 - r_2 T$ as decision rule A and equation (3.7) as decision rule B. If bargainer 1 reasons that 2, being in similar circumstances to himself, should also have arrived at the decision rule B, he realises that the rule B is no longer any good since the expectations upon which it rests (namely rule A being observed by 2) will not be fulfilled. This being so, 1 must take into account in his decisions the expectation that 2's demand will depend on his own concession rate, $-\dot{q}_1$. Without going into the details of the considerations involved, it can be seen that the reasoning will lead 1 to a decision rule C which involves choosing a function $q_1(t)$ which maximises a somewhat complicated utility functional. Since the final outcome is now recognised (by 1) to depend not just on the current demand, but on the variation of this demand over time (given by a function $q_1(t)$) the decision rule C poses a problem in the calculus of variations.

It now transpires that at least one of the bargainers must, according to a theory involving self-replacing decision rules, be deluded. It is possible that one bargainer has expectations regarding the other's decisions which are correct, but this implies that the other bargainer has expectations which are mistaken. It is also possible that both bargainers' expectations are mistaken, and this is the case which is considered in all the theories we have discussed involving self-replacing decision rules. We now turn to the demonstration of these propositions.

Suppose that bargainer 1 adopts decision rule C and bargainer 2 adopts decision rule B. This would mean that bargainer 1's expectations regarding 2's decision rule are correct, since decision rule C is based on the expectation that the other bargainer adopts decision rule B. However, decision rule B, as adopted by 2, involves the expectation that 1 has adopted decision rule A, which in the circumstances is mistaken. Also, if both bargainers adopt decision rule B (as in Cross's theory) then both have mistaken expectations, since each expects the other to be observing decision rule A.

It is clear that these results are quite general. Suppose we refer to decision rules A, B, C as 1st level, 2nd level and 3rd level rules. Then if 1 adopts an nth level rule, his expectations are only correct if 2 has adopted an $(n - 1)$th level rule. And 2's expectations are then only correct if 1 has adopted an $(n - 2)$th level rule, which is contrary to the original supposition. Hence, it follows that at least one bargainer must be mistaken in his expectations regarding the other bargainer's decision rule.

It will then be seen that, within any framework of this type, the first decision rule will always be arbitrary in the sense that it is not derived from particular lower level decision rules. Since this first decision rule plays a large part in determining the form of all the remaining higher level decision rules, it appears that its arbitrariness would constitute a serious weakness of the framework. Thus, however complicated the higher level rules become, they all rest, ultimately, on a rule which neither bargainer has any theoretical justification for adopting. (Indeed, because of the inconsistency between expectations and decisions to which it gives rise, there may be theoretical justification for not adopting it.)

However high the level of decision-making, the reasoning may always be traced back to rule A. If, in the adjustment process the bargainers could learn about the form of the other's decision rule then some of the arbitrariness would be removed. The arbitrariness would then be centred on the initial conditions (or, more precisely, the initial expectations). It must be noticed, however, that expectations cannot be eliminated altogether from the models by having a sufficiently sophisticated theory of learning (i.e. of adjustments). The decision-making will always be concerned with future events and no amount of experience can be projected into the future without some expectations (at best partially justified assumptions) about the other bargainer's behaviour.

There are, therefore, formal objections to a scheme involving self-replacing decision rules. Such a scheme entails the assumption that all the decision-makers involved expect other decision-makers to have decision rules which operate at a lower level of complexity or sophistication than their own rules. This is the formal inconsistency to which one could object. However, there is an alternative view of the situation. Whether or not a bargainer operates with an inconsistency between his own decisions and those he expects from the other bargainer is an empirical question. There is nothing self-contradictory about such an inconsistency. It merely describes or formalises a particular state of mind. It may be that, as in the example arising from Cross's theory, each bargainer follows the reasoning to higher and higher levels of decision rule until the conceptual and computational problems bring his reasoning to a stop. Here we are appealing, as Simon does,[1] to the limited intelligence available for decision-making processes in real organisms. Thus, it is feasible that different bargainers come to rest at different levels of decision rule, although it will be noticed that all the existing theories we have considered confine their attention to the case where both bargainers come to rest at the same level. In this case each bargainer is mistaken about the form of the other's decision rule, as we have shown. It would therefore be interesting to consider the case where the bargainers operate on different levels of decision rule in such a way that one of them has correct expectations about the form of the other's decision rule. Within the example considered previously, this could happen in one of two ways. Either 1 could adopt rule C and 2 rule B, or 1 could adopt rule B and 2 rule A. In either

---

[1] H. A. Simon, 'A Behavioral Model of Rational Choice,' *Quarterly Journal of Economics*, 69, 1955, pp. 99–118. This point is considered further in Chapter V.

case bargainer 1 would correctly anticipate the form of 2's decision rule.

Regarding the analysis of these two cases, the first one cannot be dealt with since the decision rule C (involving the choice, at each instant, of a function $q_1(t)$ which maximises a utility functional), would be far too complicated to handle, mathematically. The second case is mathematically straightforward but rather uninteresting as will be seen. Here, bargainer 2 adopts rule A which can be written

(4.2) $$q_2 = q_2^0 - R_2 T$$

where R_2 is the constant concession rate chosen by 2. Bargainer 1, on the other hand, correctly anticipating that 2 is adopting this rule, is following decision rule B, which could be referred to as the Cross rule. Bargainer 1's demand is then given by

(4.3) $$q_1 = \frac{r_2}{a_1}$$

where

(4.4) $$\dot{r}_2 = \alpha_1(-\dot{q}_2 - r_2).$$

However, since $\dot{q}_2 = -R_2$, we have upon integration

$$r_2 = R_2 + (r_2^0 - R_2)e^{-\alpha_1 T}$$

where r_2^0 is the value of r_2 at $T = 0$. Hence, 1's demands are given by

(4.5) $$q_1 = \frac{R_2}{a_1} + \frac{1}{a_1}(r_2^0 - R_2)e^{-\alpha_1 T}.$$

If $r_2^0 > R_2$, q_1 decreases over time, i.e. bargainer 1 concedes. This is the case shown in Figure 4.1. The time of agreement T is the value of T which satisfies $q_1 + q_2 = M$. As far as the actual agreement is concerned, (ignoring for the moment the time at which it is reached) it is always to bargainer 2's

65

advantage to have smaller values of R_2. This follows from the fact that

$$(4.6) \qquad \frac{\partial q_1}{\partial R_2} = \frac{1}{a_1}(1 - e^{-\alpha_1 T}) > 0 \text{ for } T > 0.$$

If $R_2 = 0$ then bargainer 1 does all the conceding. The time at which agreement is reached will also depend on R_2. This might lead us to consider how bargainer 2 could choose an optimal value of R_2, but such considerations have no real significance. In his decision-making, bargainer 2 does not do anything as involved as discount expected future benefits. The only way we

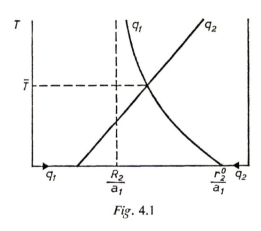

Fig. 4.1

can make any sense of the formalism is to regard 2 as a kind of bargaining simpleton who just gives in as time elapses. If bargainer 2 concedes at a sufficiently great rate, so that $R_2 > r_2^0$, bargainer 1 will retract his initial offer and move asymptotically towards the demand R_2/a_1. It is not worthwhile pursuing this analysis in any detail since the mechanism of the model is evidently not very interesting. Although bargainer 1 responds to 2's behaviour, 2 is completely impervious to the behaviour of 1. Hence there is no real interaction in the model, only a one way flow of causation. In the higher level models with asymmetrical decision-making, genuine interaction would be present.

Unfortunately, the analysis of such models would involve mathematics a long way beyond the scope of this work.

4. DECISION-MAKING AND EXPECTATIONS IN A GAME THEORY MODEL

We now put forward a very simple game model of the bargaining process. This consists of a non-cooperative non-zero-sum game in which each player has a choice between only two strategies. Although this formulation will, of course, avoid all the most

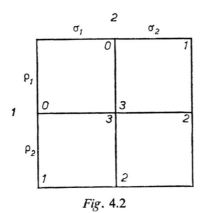

Fig. 4.2

interesting tactical questions, it seems to capture at least something of the spirit of the situation. The game is illustrated in Figure 4.2.

In the figure, ρ_1 and σ_1 may each be interpreted as the strategy 'be intransigent' and ρ_2 and σ_2 may each be interpreted as the strategy 'make concessions'. If both bargainers decide to be intransigent (ρ_1, σ_1), they end up with no agreement, to the disadvantage of both. If one has decided to make concessions while the other has decided to be intransigent (ρ_1, σ_2), (ρ_2, σ_1) they both do better than they would with no agreement, but it is to each one's advantage to be the intransigent one of the pair. If each decided to make concessions (ρ_2, σ_2), each does better

67

than making concessions to an intransigent opponent, but not as well as being intransigent with a conceding opponent.

We consider now the decision problem faced by bargainer 1 and, in particular, the relationship between his decisions and his expectations of 2's decisions. If 1 expects 2 to choose the strategy σ_2 (make concessions), this leads 1 to choose the strategy ρ_1 (be intransigent). Also, if 1 expects 2 to choose the strategy σ_1 this leads 1 to choose the strategy ρ_2. A similar state of affairs exists for bargainer 2. Clearly, either decision, to concede or to be intransigent, is self-replacing in the same sense that we have considered decision rules to be self-replacing in the previous discussion.

Formally, this situation corresponds with the fact that the game has two equilibrium pairs (ρ_1,σ_2) and (ρ_2,σ_1) which are neither equivalent nor interchangeable.[1] Two equilibrium pairs are equivalent if the payoff to each player is the same for each pair. Thus (ρ,σ) and (ρ',σ') are equivalent if $v_1(\rho,\sigma) = v_1(\rho',\sigma')$ and $v_2(\rho,\sigma) = v_2(\rho',\sigma')$, where $v_1(\eta,\theta)$, $v_2(\eta,\theta)$ are the payoffs to players 1 and 2 respectively resulting from the pair of strategy choices (η,θ). These two pairs are interchangeable if (ρ,σ') and (ρ',σ) are also equilibrium pairs.[2] It can be seen that the existence of equilibrium pairs which are not equivalent entails a conflict of interest among these pairs. The existence of equilibrium pairs which are not interchangeable entails a problem of coordination among them.

What are the implications of this discussion? It is clear that in practice bargainers do choose between making concessions and following an intransigent path. Yet strategic reasoning in a situation where the decisions are self-replacing is fraught with circularity and does not give rise to any solutions. The fact that the bare structure of payoffs involved does not suggest which choice will be made by each bargainer seems to reflect, if

---

[1] It is only in zero-sum games that equilibrium pairs can be guaranteed to be equivalent and interchangeable. See R. D. Luce and H. Raiffa, *Games and Decisions*, J. Wiley & Sons, New York, 1957, pp. 66, 90–1.

[2] *Ibid.* p. 90.

anything, the poverty of this formalisation. It may be that when one play of the game is regarded as part of a whole series of plays, much of the indeterminacy is removed. In the longer run, patterns may be established and some form of tacit coordination achieved.[1] (This possibility appears to correspond to the existence of initial expectations in models within the decision/expectation/adjustment framework.) It is suggested again in Chapter V that many bargaining processes may only be fully understood as a part of a longer-term bargaining relationship.

5. LIMITATIONS OF THE ENVIRONMENT CONCEPT

We are now in a position to suggest what might be the limitations of the environment concept which was introduced in Chapter I to aid in the analysis of the decisions of each bargainer. We have shown that when the environment becomes a single decision-maker in the same circumstances as the decision-maker under consideration, questions of consistency arise. The decision-maker may carry out all kinds of reasoning about the environment but the possibility always arises that the environment may equally well be carrying out the same reasoning about him. This possibility does not arise when the environment consists of many decision-makers since there is no reason to suppose that an aggregate of decision-makers behaves in the same way as a single decision-maker. Indeed, by appealing to the laws of large numbers we may fairly safely assume that an aggregate of decision-makers will have a simpler and more stable set of responses to changing circumstances than any of the individual decision-makers within the aggregate.

Thus, when the environment is composed of a single decision-maker, the possibility of self-replacing decision rules arises,

[1] See A. Rapoport and A. M. Chammah, *Prisoner's Dilemma*, University of Michigan Press, Ann Arbor, 1965, for an extensive development of this idea together with many experimental results. This work, however, is based on the prisoner's dilemma game rather than the bargaining game considered here.

these in turn leading to an infinite regress of possible arguments about how the environment behaves. It seems that in extending the environment concept to cover small group processes, one encounters quite distinctive problems. It has been our purpose here to show that these problems are not merely the technical difficulties of developing a sophisticated enough system of actions to represent the environment's responses to the decision-maker's possible actions, but rather that they are difficulties which reside in the logic of the situation.

Chater V

DIFFERENT APPROACHES TO A
THEORY OF BARGAINING

---

1. INTRODUCTION

The theory of games has been widely used as a basis for attempts to construct a theory of the bargaining process.[1] In this chapter we wish to consider the limitations of the game-theoretic approach to bargaining processes and, in the light of this discussion, to show how the present framework provides a quite different form of approach. It may then be possible to see what limitations are overcome by this decision/expectation/adjustment model and what limitations are still inherent in it.

2. GAME THEORY AS A BASIS FOR A THEORY OF BARGAINING

A two-person game model (in normal form) consists of two sets of strategies $R = \{\rho_1, \rho_2, \ldots \rho_n\}$, $S = \{\sigma_1, \sigma_2 \ldots \sigma_m\}$ the first being the strategies available to player 1 and the second being those available to player 2. With each pair of strategies ρ_i, σ_j, one from each set, is associated an outcome O_{ij}. Each outcome then has associated with it a pair of utilities $v_1(\rho_i, \sigma_j)$, $v_2(\rho_i, \sigma_j)$ representing the values of the outcome O_{ij} to the players 1 and 2 respectively. The situation can then be represented by a table as shown in Figure 5.1. A game then consists of player 1 choosing a strategy from the set R and, simultaneously and in ignorance of player 1's choice, player 2 choosing a strategy from the set S.

---

[1] See R. L. Bishop, 'Game Theoretic Analyses of Bargaining,' *Quarterly Journal of Economics*, 77, 1963, pp. 559–602.

Traditionally, games have been divided into two kinds according to the manner in which the choice of strategies is made. In this way the distinction between cooperative and non-cooperative games arose. In a cooperative game the players have complete freedom of preplay communication to make joint binding agreements. In a non-cooperative game no preplay communication is permitted between the players.

According to this distinction a bargaining process is modelled as a cooperative game, so that the actual negotiating appears

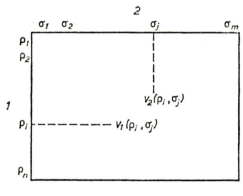

Fig. 5.1

within the model as preplay communication. However, if one goes back a stage further, each player must choose how he will negotiate, so that if one includes negotiation as part of the 'play' of the game, the game becomes non-cooperative. The distinction between cooperative and non-cooperative is not inherent in the situation, but depends on the way the situation is modelled.[1] Since we are concerned in this work with the negotiations by means of which a bargain may be struck, it will be appropriate to regard the negotiation process as a part of

---

[1] As Schelling has argued (T. C. Schelling, *The Strategy of Conflict,* Oxford University Press, New York, 1963, p. 99), 'non-cooperative' is in any case a rather misleading term for non-zero-sum games where communication is not permitted.

the game itself, rather than as preplay communication.[1] Thus, contrary to usual practice, the bargaining situation will be represented by a non-cooperative game model. The strategies ρ_i, σ_j then consist not just of demands for particular outcomes (as they would in the cooperative model of the situation) but of whole negotiating strategies. A particular strategy, ρ_i, would contain a complete set of instructions for carrying the process through to its conclusion, i.e., a list of what to do initially and how to respond to each possible contingency.

A. Solution concepts in non-zero-sum game theory

Since the bargainers have a mutual interest in reaching some agreement within the contract zone, the bargaining process must be represented by a non-zero-sum game. If the situation were to be represented by a zero-sum game there would have to be no mutual preferences of the bargainers among the outcomes. Now, although there is a theory of zero-sum games which comes to quite definite conclusions about the behaviour of rational players, no corresponding state of affairs exists in the theory of non-zero-sum games. Luce and Raiffa[2] discuss the following solution concepts for non-cooperative non-zero-sum games:

(1) solution in the sense of Nash;
(2) solution in the strict sense;
(3) solution in the weak sense;
(4) solution in the complete weak sense.

A discussion of the nature and rationale of the different solution concepts would take us very far from the question at issue.[3] The point we wish to make is that there is an embarrassing profusion of solutions to a non-zero-sum game. So, even if it

---

[1] See R. D. Luce and H. Raiffa, *Games and Decisions*, J. Wiley & Sons, New York, 1957, p. 113.
[2] *Ibid.* pp. 106–9.
[3] *Ibid.* pp. 106–10.

were practicable to set up a model in this way (i.e. if the number of possible strategies involved could be handled), game theory would not be much help to us in our efforts to discover how supposedly rational bargainers would behave. The various solution concepts listed above are all ways of selecting some pairs (if they exist) from the set of all equilibrium pairs of strategies of the game. Here p_{i_0}, σ_{j_0} is defined to be an equilibrium pair provided no outcome O_{ij_0} is preferred by 1 to $O_{i_0 j_0}$ and no outcome $O_{i_0 j}$ is preferred by 2 to $O_{i_0 j_0}$. Thus, whatever the

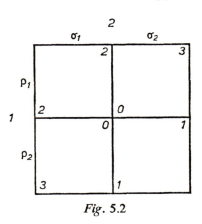

Fig. 5.2

special features of each of the different solution concepts, they all rest on the idea of equilibrium pairs. But although the equilibrium pairs have the interesting property that each strategy in the pair is the best against the other, it can still be contested whether this property is very important where non-zero-sum games are concerned. For example, in the well-known prisoner's dilemma game, illustrated in Figure 5.2, there is a unique equilibrium pair at (p_2, σ_2).[1] But experimental games[2] have shown that many players choose (p_1, σ_1) and of course, by

[1] A. Rapoport, *Fights, Games and Debates,* University of Michigan Press, Ann Arbor, 1960, pp. 173–4.
[2] A. Rapoport and Carol Orwant, 'Experimental Games: A Review,' in *Game Theory and Related Approaches to Social Behavior* edited by M. Shubik, J. Wiley & Sons, New York, 1964, Chapter 20.

doing so they are much better off than two players who seek the equilibrium pair.

Even if it is admitted that there is no general theory of non-zero-sum games, it may still be that at a less ambitious level one may be able to develop a theory of particular classes of non-zero-sum games. Thus, although the theory may have nothing very satisfactory to say about non-zero-sum games in general, it could still be that a game theory framework is a useful starting point in the analysis of the particular class of bargaining games. Bearing in mind the rather disjointed state of affairs which exists in regard to the non-zero-sum solution concepts, we must still go on to consider game theory as a classificatory framework, supposing that particular cases of the framework may be put to some explanatory use.

B. The concept of a strategy and the sequential aspects of the game

It will be argued here that by taking the concept of a strategy as the basis of the analysis in game theory, the sequential aspects of the situation become effectively buried. In choosing a strategy a player must arrive at a set of instructions telling him what to do in every possible contingency. In the case of a bargaining process, the bargainers would arrive at the bargaining table with their minds fully made up and the whole process predetermined. It is then only a matter of going through the motions. In fact there would be no real need for them to meet at all. A third party could work out the outcome if the two bargainers sent their strategies to him.

Within this framework the dynamics of the process are lost to view. The whole series of interactions leading to some outcome are collapsed inside the strategies and they remain there as long as the strategy concept is the basis of the framework. In order to avoid this one may convert the game from normal form to extensive form, representing the situation by a game tree. But the fruitfulness of game theory lies in the insights it provides into the nature of the strategic reasoning appropriate to the structure of the payoffs as revealed by the normal form of the game. By putting the game into extensive form the sequential aspects are restored to view but the special virtues of game theoretic reasoning are lost.

It is here that a point made by Simon seems appropriate.[1] Simon has argued that in human decision-makers the extent of knowledge regarding the environment and the computational facilities are distinctly limited. Thus, Simon was led to suppose that decision-making by mortals is far more localised and myopic than would be predicted by a theory of global optimising under conditions of perfect knowledge. This argument, it seems, can be directed against game theory models with some force. For here the number of possible strategies in any tolerably realistic model would be astronomical.

C. *Assumptions regarding the knowledge of the players*

In game theory each player is supposed to know not only his own utilities for the various outcomes but the other player's as well. Furthermore, if mixed strategies are to be considered, the utilities concerned must be cardinal measures, i.e. they must be determined up to a positive linear transformation. This is a stronger measure than an ordering of preferences which is only determined up to any monotonic transformation. This is no place to resurrect the ordinalist versus cardinalist controversy and in fact all we wish to point out is what considerable intellectual strain is imposed on the players if they are to be anything like as well informed as their theoretical counterparts. In terms of Simon's argument, game theory supposes that each player has perfect global knowledge of his own and the other's cardinal preferences, and that such knowledge arises at no cost to the players. If, in bargaining processes, the decision-maker's knowledge-gathering facilities are at all limited and if knowledge

[1] H. A. Simon, 'A Behavioral Model of Rational Choice,' *Quarterly Journal of Economics*, 69, 1955, pp. 99–118.

is not in practice freely available, then the game theory model would seem to give a somewhat misleading picture of the situation.

3. THE DECISION/EXPECTATION/ADJUSTMENT APPROACH

It will be pointed out here exactly how this approach differs from the approach offered by the theory of games.

First, we make the somewhat trivial point that this approach involves no difficulties with different solution concepts. The 'solution' is simply the agreement which is finally arrived at, if any.

Second, we must enquire what has happened to the concept of a strategy in moving from game theory to this framework. In doing this we may consider the two frameworks in a purely formal way, leaving aside the detailed interpretation of the formalisms. In game theory a strategy involves sufficient information for a player to carry out the whole process, i.e. a set of instructions for playing one whole game. In the decision/expectation/adjustment approach a 'strategy' would be defined by a set of values of a_i, γ_i and V_{ij}^0 (the initial value of V_{ij}). Each different set of values of a_i, γ_i and V_{ij}^0 would describe a possible strategy in the game theory sense. But this equivalence is only a formal matter. When we come to look at the interpretation placed on the formalism, we see that there is a very fundamental difference between the two approaches. For the whole point of game theory is that each player is free to choose one of the possible strategies. In the other approach, however, because there is a higher degree of parametrisation than in game theory, the bargainer's strategy is, as it were, built into him. It is just a fact of the bargainer's mode of behaviour that he discounts future benefits at the rate a_i and there is no choice involved in this value. A similar state of affairs exists with regard to the values of γ_i and V_{ij}^0. Since the strategies are not consciously chosen there is no reason to suppose that they have any optimal or equilibrium properties.

For convenience, we may refer to a bargainer who behaves according to the decision/expectation/adjustment scheme as a Cross-type bargainer. It is clear that a Cross-type bargainer makes choices. He chooses what he believes to be an optimal demand in the light of his current expectations. But we notice that the demand which the bargainer believes to be optimal is in fact derived from what are in general mistaken expectations.[1] Hence the decision which is made will be an imperfect optimum (i.e. it is optimal with respect to the limited, imperfect knowledge available to the bargainer), in contrast to the optima of game theory which are based on perfect knowledge and unlimited computational powers. The Cross-type bargainer makes decisions based on his immediate expectations without allowing for the future changes which will take place in them. Whereas the bargainer of the game theory model is concerned with strategy, the Cross-type bargainer is involved with tactics.

We can now see how the present approach meets Simon's objections to models involving global rationality, i.e. rationality based on perfect knowledge and unlimited computational powers. For the knowledge possessed by a Cross-type bargainer is limited as are his computational powers. (For example, in the Cross theory itself, each bargainer neglects the fact that changes in his own demand will affect the other bargainer's concession rate.) Although the Cross-type bargainer makes maximising rather than satisficing decisions, this seems unimportant compared with the fact that his decisions are imperfect rather than global optima.[2] The Cross-type bargainer would seem to make choices in accordance with '. . . definitions

---

[1] Even in the case where bargainer 1 uses a decision rule of one level higher than bargainer 2, so that the form of 1's expectations are correct, the parameter(s) involved, such as V_{ij}, will not in general be initially correct. It is only as the adjustments proceed that the parameter(s) in 1's expectations will tend towards the correct value(s).

[2] Indeed, one could argue that satisficing decisions could always be converted into maximising terms by including appropriate costs of increasing the accuracy of the decision. The distinction then becomes a matter of style.

of "rational choice" that are modelled more closely upon the actual decision processes in the behavior of organisms. . .'.[1]

If we consider the inherent parameters of his behaviour, the Cross-type bargainer arrives at the bargaining table with a strategy in the game theory sense. But if we consider also the way in which the model is interpreted, the bargainer does not choose a strategy at all: he makes short run or myopic choices which lead him to inexorably follow the strategy with which he has been endowed. The present framework therefore corresponds to what Rapoport has termed a 'cataclysmic' as opposed to a 'strategic' model of conflict.[2] Rapoport has argued that these two types of model are complementary to one another in our understanding of conflict processes, each model giving emphasis to one aspect of conflict in reality. Whereas the strategic models (like those of game theory) give all the emphasis to the freedom of choice and the control that decision-makers may have over the process, the cataclysmic models (like Cross's model and the present framework) give emphasis to the built-in dynamics of the process before which the decision-maker is powerless. It seems likely that all conflict situations in reality have some inner dynamics which can only be accepted but at the same time leave some room for active choice.

Lastly we will consider the assumptions in this approach regarding the knowledge of the bargainers. We notice that whereas in game theory the decisions of a player depend on both his own and the other's utilities, in this approach the decisions of a bargainer are based on his own utilities. The decisions are, of course, also influenced by the bargainer's expectations regarding the behaviour of the other bargainer and any knowledge of the other bargainer's utilities may influence this. More plausibly, however, the expectations may be

[1] H. A. Simon, 'A Behavioral Model of Rational Choice,' *Quarterly Journal of Economics*, 69, 1955, p. 114.

[2] A. Rapoport, 'Models of Conflict: Cataclysmic and Strategic,' presented at the Symposium 'Conflict in Society,' The CIBA Foundation, London, 1965.

based on previous experience of bargaining processes rather than on anything as imponderable as the other bargainer's cardinal preferences. A theory of the bargaining relationship would include as explained variables factors which are un-explained parameters within a single bargaining process. Indeed, some very familiar concepts like 'loss of face' may only be understood from a theoretical point of view by considering the long term effect of one bargainer's present actions on the other bargainer's expectations in future bargaining processes. At the theoretical level, the longer-run aspects of bargaining processes are completely unexplored. While at the more practical level labour economists have pointed out the impor-tance of these long-run consequences of current actions, theorists have been wholly concerned with the problem of constructing a theory of a single bargaining process. A theory of the bargaining relationship has yet to be developed.

Chapter VI

FURTHER DEVELOPMENTS

1. INTRODUCTION

The object of this chapter is to return to a consideration of the framework which was set forth in Chapter I and which was briefly touched upon in Chapter III in connection with Cross's theory. At this stage we will attempt to bring these threads together and make some theoretical explorations within the framework. In the course of these explorations much greater attention than has been previously given will be devoted to the workings of the adjustment process. The analysis will suggest that there are certain limitations on the combinations of assumptions one can make (within the present framework) about the bargainers' behaviour. Following this discussion there is a numerical solution of an illustrative bargaining model.

2. A NON-LINEAR ASSUMPTION

The concern first will be with assumption (II) in Chapter III: the assumption of linear expectations[1] (see p. 49). The discussion will lead us to consider also assumption (I): the assumption of independence. What we wish to show is that the assumption of linearity of expectations does not seem consonant with the structure of the situation. Following from this it will be pointed out that without the linear expectations a rather different form

---

[1] The author has dealt elsewhere with other aspects of the restrictiveness of this assumption. See A. Coddington, 'A Theory of the Bargaining Process: Comment,' *American Economic Review*, 56, 1966, pp. 522–30.

of adjustment process can take place,[1] exhibiting an additional form of interdependence between the two bargainers.

If one bargainer expects that the other's demand will vary linearly with future time, it follows that he expects to be able to achieve any agreement whatsoever by simply waiting long enough. In particular, it follows that he expects to be able to achieve agreements outside the contract zone within some finite time. But as a matter of definition it follows that no bargainer would want to settle for any agreement outside the contract zone. It appears, therefore, that the linear expectations do not adequately reflect the constraints on the outcome of the process.[2] It may, of course, be argued that when it comes to a situation of serious, hard bargaining, where the amount of disagreement separating the bargainers is small compared with the width of the contract zone, then the linear assumption constitutes a very useful approximation. However, in the present work, concerned as we are with explorations and developments of the framework, we will try to show some possible theoretical consequences of relaxing the linearity assumption. In this way we would no longer need an assumption that we are concerned with a case of hard bargaining. The theory would then have some relevance to a situation in which the amount of disagreement is not small compared with the width of the contract zone. Thus, it might be said that we are trying to develop a theory which includes the case of tentative or exploratory bargaining.

With the assumption of linear expectations, the variation of the expected time of agreement, t_i^* with q_i, bargainer i's current demand, is given by (3.6). Relaxing this assumption

---

[1] It will transpire that it is not the linearity itself which makes the difference but the fact that the linear functions of q_i, q_j are separable.

[2] As Cross himself points out (J. G. Cross, 'A Theory of the Bargaining Process,' *American Economic Review*, 55, 1965, p. 89), in his model the demands are quite liable to go outside the contract zone, while his theory only operates when the demands have come within it. It will become apparent that this difficulty can be overcome by introducing suitable non-linear functions in the theory of expectations.

we now list a set of conditions which a non-linear dependence of t_i^* on q_i would have to satisfy if it is to be considered consonant with the structure of the situation.

(6.1)
$$t_i^* = 0 \text{ for } q_i \leq M - q_j$$
$$t_i^* \to \infty \text{ for } q_i \to M$$
$$t_i^* = \text{is undefined for } q_i > M$$
$$\frac{\delta t_i^*}{\delta q_i} > 0$$

The first condition expresses the idea that bargainer i can settle for j's current offer, $M - q_j$, immediately. The second and third conditions express the idea that bargainer i expects that there could never be an agreement outside the contract zone. The fourth condition expresses the idea that each bargainer expects that agreements more favourable to himself take longer to achieve.

Suppose there is a function

(6.2)
$$t_i^* = L(V_{ij}, q_i, q_j, M)$$

which satisfies the conditions (6.1). Since we suppose that M is constant in any bargaining process, we may omit any mention of it in the future. It will now be shown that, within the context of the present assumptions, a further restriction must be made on (6.2) in addition to the conditions (6.1).

Having set $C_i = 0$ in equation (3.4), the utility function now takes the form

(6.3)
$$u_i = u_i(q_i) \, e^{-a_i t_i^*}.$$

The theory of decision-making then arises by supposing that bargainer i chooses the value of q_i which maximises this function. Differentiating with respect to q_i and supposing that the second order condition for a maximum is satisfied, this means that the bargainer makes the demand q_i which satisfies

(6.4)
$$u_i'(q_i) = a_i L_2(V_{ij}, q_i, q_j) u_i(q_i),$$

83

where $L_k(V_{ij}, q_i, q_j)$ denotes the partial derivative of L with respect to its kth independent variable.[1] If it is remembered that this partial derivative is in general a function of V_{ij}, q_i and q_j, it will be convenient to denote it by $\dfrac{\partial t_i^*}{\partial q_i}$. This decision-making theory is illustrated in Figure 6.1. The q_i which satisfies

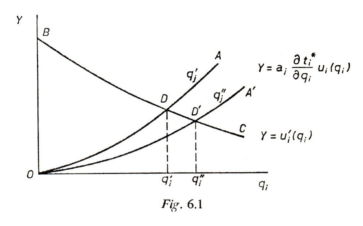

Fig. 6.1

(6.4) may be thought of as the solution of the pair of simultaneous equations

(6.5)
$$Y = a_i \frac{\partial t_i^*}{\partial q_i} u_i(q_i)$$

$$Y = u_i'(q_i).$$

These are shown as OA and BC respectively in the figure.

---

[1] In fact the first order condition for a maximum should involve the total derivative

$$\frac{dL}{dq_i} = L_1 \frac{\partial V_{ij}}{\partial q_i} + L_2 + L_3 \frac{\partial q_j}{\partial q_i}.$$

However, the independence assumption allows bargainer i to suppose $\partial q_j/\partial q_i = 0$ and, when applied to equation (1.11), this same assumption allows him to suppose that $\partial V_{ij}/\partial q_i = 0$. In other words, the independence assumption makes it possible to use the partial derivative in place of the total derivative.

BC has been drawn as a strictly decreasing function by the assumption of diminishing marginal utility. We do not have sufficient assumptions to determine whether OA is an increasing or decreasing function. However, if an optimal demand is to exist there must be an intersection between the curves OA and BC. Therefore, since $u_i(0) = 0$, OA must be increasing over some region if it is to intersect the marginal gains curve which, we may suppose, never reaches zero. For simplicity, we therefore show OA as a strictly increasing function.

The decision-making theory may be interpreted in the following way. There are gains to be expected from demanding greater values of q_i, but on the other hand there are time costs to be expected in attaining these more favourable outcomes. The current demand is (subjectively) optimal when the expected marginal gain is equal to the expected marginal time costs. The marginal utility curve BC represents the expected marginal gains and the curve OA may be thought of as representing the expected marginal time costs associated with a current demand, q_i. The point of intersection of these curves, D, determines the q_i which satisfies the marginal condition.

It can be seen that, since $\dfrac{\partial t_i^*}{\partial q_i}$ is in general a function of q_j, a change in bargainer j's demand will cause the curve OA to shift, even with V_{ij} held constant. If j decreases his demand from q_j' to q_j'' the intersection shifts from D to D', say, and i increases his demand from q_i' to q_i''. This reasoning only applies, however, when V_{ij} is held constant and so does not give the complete picture. A change in q_j will usually have other repercussions via the adjustment of expectations. In other words, when q_j changes, this will in general give rise to a revision of the value of V_{ij} causing a further shift of the curve OA. Therefore we cannot say, at this stage, whether the *resultant* change in q_i caused by a decrease in q_j will be an increase or a decrease. That is, if all the repercussions are taken into account, it is not yet apparent whether a concession from j will be reciprocated or will lead i to make an increased demand.

Two forms of interdependence can now be recognised in the decision-making theory. The first form of interdependence arises because of the existence of q_j in the equation (6.4). We may call this 'direct interdependence' since it arises because of the influence of j's current decision on i's current decision. The second form arises because of the existence of V_{ij} in equation (6.4). Following Fellner,[1] we may call this 'conjectural interdependence' since it arises from the influence on i's decisions of his expectations regarding j's behaviour. Cross's theory, because of the linear form of the variation of t_i^* with q_i (equation (3.6)) gives rise to a $\dfrac{\partial t_i^*}{\partial q_i}$ which is independent of q_j, so missing any kind of direct interdependence and being concerned exclusively with the conjectural form.

3. THE ADJUSTMENT PROCESS

As time elapses, conditions change and decisions are revised. It is to this adjustment process that attention will now be given.

Corresponding to the two forms of interdependence we have distinguished, there are two forms of adjustment. The first form of adjustment consists of changes in q_i directly brought about by changes in q_j.[2] These can be termed 'direct adjustments'. The second form of adjustment consists of changes in q_i brought about by changes in the expectation variable V_{ij}. These can be termed 'conjectural adjustments'. Notice, however, that the separation of the two forms of adjustment is an analytical device: in reality both forms of adjustment will have a simultaneous effect on the revision of q_i.

[1] W. J. Fellner, *Competition Among the Few*, Knopf, New York, 1949, p. 14.
[2] The qualification 'directly' must be inserted since changes in q_j in general cause changes in V_{ij} which in turn cause changes in q_i. Therefore conjectural adjustments also involve changes in q_i brought about by changes in q_j, but by an indirect process.

A. *Direct adjustments*

It can be seen that, for a given value of V_{ij}, equation (6.4) defines an implicit functional relation between q_i and q_j. Suppose that this relation is written as:

(6.6) $\mu_i(q_i,q_j) = 0, \quad i \neq j.$

There is, therefore, one function μ_1 denoting the dependence of the choice of q_1 on q_2 and a second function μ_2 denoting the dependence of the choice of q_2 on q_1. This situation may be represented by curves in the q_1, q_2 plane as shown in Figure 6.2.

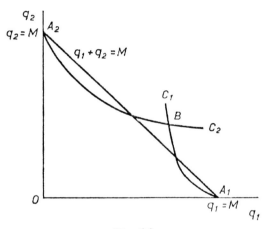

Fig. 6.2

Here, A_1BC_1 represents the choice of q_1 and A_2BC_2 the choice of q_2. It follows from the assumptions (6.1) that the curves A_1BC_1 and A_2BC_2 are of the form shown, ending on the points (M, O) and (O, M) respectively. In Cross's theory the corresponding construction would involve a horizontal and a vertical line in the q_1, q_2 plane, since, from equation (3.7) representing Cross's decision theory, the choice of q_i is independent of the value of q_j. This is shown in Figure 6.3 where D_1EF_1 represents the choice of q_1 and D_2EF_2 represents the choice of q_2. (The positions of the lines D_1EF_1 and D_2EF_2 will, of course, depend on the values of r_2 and r_1 respectively.)

87

The decision theory as developed so far implies that bargainer 1 chooses demands along the curve A_1BC_1 and bargainer 2 chooses demands along A_2BC_2. The only point at which the demands are consistent with one another is at the point B. This point can be referred to as the equilibrium point of the direct adjustment process. In fact we will consider here only an equilibrium theory of the direct adjustment process. We will suppose that as the curves A_1BC_1, A_2BC_2 shift due to the conjectural adjustments (i.e. due to changes in V_{12} and V_{21}) the

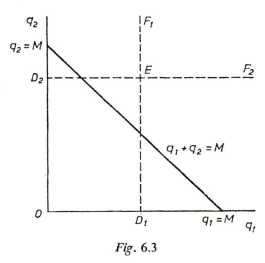

Fig. 6.3

demands of the bargainers are always at the equilibrium point B. In other words, we give no account of how the demands adjust to reach B. The dynamics of the direct adjustment process will be ignored, but it will transpire that these have no consequences for the present discussion. The dynamics of the conjectural adjustments will, however, be considered and these will be represented by the motion of the point B in the q_1, q_2 plane as the curves A_1BC_1, A_2BC_2 shift due to the variation of V_{12} and V_{21}. The motion of the point B then continues until such time (if any) as it reaches the line $q_1 + q_2 = M$ which is the locus of all possible points of agreement. We cannot discuss the actual shifts of the curves A_1BC_1, A_2BC_2 until we have a theory of how V_{ij} changes in response to i's experience of j's behaviour. It is to this topic of conjectural adjustments we now turn.

B. Conjectural adjustments

The general problem here is how a bargainer would use the actual series of values of q_j over time, T, to modify his expectations $E_i(T)\{q_j(t)\}$ over future time, t. Clearly the two curves q_j against T and $E_i(T)\{q_j(t)\}$ against t must coincide at the

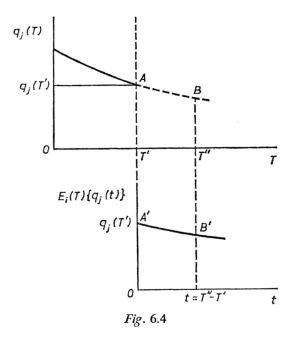

Fig. 6.4

present moment, T, i.e. at $t = 0$. This is a necessary condition which $E_i(T)\{q_j(t)\}$ must fulfill if it is to make sense as a set of expectations. However, the present moment is also the point at which the two curves may be compared, since one exists only for $t \leqslant 0$ and the other only for $t \geqslant 0$. This is illustrated in Figure 6.4 which shows the situation at a time T'. As time elapses the lower set of axes moves from left to right so that the

89

origin $t = 0$ is always below the point on the T axis which represents the present moment.

If it is supposed, as it was in Chapter I, that adjustments of expectations may be represented by the changes in a single variable, V_{ij}, then all that is required for a theory of conjectural adjustments is a single condition which V_{ij} must satisfy. Since $E_i(T)\{q_j(t)\}_{t=0}$ and $q_j(T)$ are necessarily equal at all times, T, no adjustments can be made by comparing expected with actual demands at each present moment. However, V_{ij} could be adjusted by making a comparison between $\frac{d}{dt} E_i(T)\{q_j(t)\}_{t=0}$ and $\frac{d}{dT} q_j(T)$, i.e. between the expected and the actual rates of concession. Following this line of thought then leads to an assumption like (1.11).

A number of points should be made concerning the restrictiveness of this type of assumption. First, it can be seen that the bargainer can never adjust the actual form of the expectations. He must confine himself, within this theory, to making shifts which can be represented by the changes in value of one variable, V_{ij}. Presumably, in a more realistic model, it would be possible for a bargainer to learn that the expectations were not of the form he anticipated and make adjustments accordingly. But this would involve the existence of a number of adjustment variables some of which may be constant in the shorter run, but which may change in the longer run if the expectations are to achieve a different form. However, when there is a number of adjustment variables, the distinction between the form and level of expectations becomes unclear. The formalisation and analysis of such a type of adjustment process would indeed be a formidable task.

The second point is closely related to the first. This concerns the possibility of making adjustments by comparing current and previous demands, q_j, with past expectations. Returning to Figure 6.4, suppose that the present time is T''. The bargainer may then make adjustments of his expectations by comparing his expectations at the previous time T', with the actual series of demands in the intervening period, i.e. he may make adjustments at T'' by comparing the curve $A'B'$ (representing past expectations) with the curve AB. Again, such possibilities raise formidable analytical difficulties.

The fact that the bargainer makes adjustments only in response to the values of variables at the present moment does not mean that he is unaffected by past values of variables. The value of $V_{ij}(T')$ is determined by all the preceding values of $q_j(T)$. The fact that the adjustments are instantaneous does not imply that the bargainers have no memory but that the relevant contents of each one's memory can be collapsed into a single figure, V_{ij}. Greater realism can be achieved again only at the expense of introducing a number of adjustment variables rather than a single one.

A final point concerns the pure intransigence assumption. Within the context of this assumption, each bargainer may make adjustments to his expectations regarding the other's behaviour, but he never makes adjustments to his expectations regarding his own behaviour. No matter how many concessions he may have made, he always expects that he is going to be perfectly intransigent from then onwards. We retain this assumption since it does seem to capture, however approximately, an important aspect of 'bargaining mentality'. However, we now go on to show how this imposes restrictions on the other assumptions within the model.

4. DIRECT INTERDEPENDENCE AND THE CONSISTENCY OF DECISIONS

Here we are concerned with one type of consistency within the models, namely the consistency between the same bargainer's decisions at different points in time. In Chapter IV a different type of consistency is examined, this being the consistency between a bargainer's decision-making and his expectations regarding the other bargainer's decision-making.

If a bargainer's expectations are fulfilled we would suppose that he would not revise the decision which rested on those expectations. If this supposition is correct we may say that the bargainer's decisions exhibit consistency over time. This idea will now be examined in connection with the model which has been developed here.

Suppose that bargainer 1's expectation of 2's future demands is given by AB in Figure 6.5. The exact form of AB is unimpor-

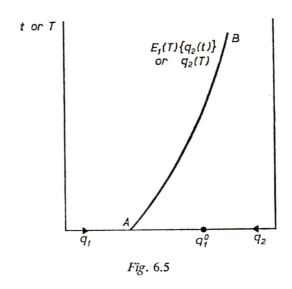

Fig. 6.5

tant for the present considerations. Suppose also that there is direct interdependence between the demands of the two bargainers. This implies, in particular, that 1's current demand depends on 2's current demand as indicated by equation (6.4) with $i = 1$ and $j = 2$. Of course, due to the existence of conjectural interdependence, 1's current demand also depends on his expectations, this form of dependence being represented by the variable V_{ij} in (6.4). Since the exact form of dependence is immaterial for the present discussion we can write 1's demand as

(6.7) $$q_1 = \lambda_1(q_2, V_{12}).$$

92

We may suppose that AB is the particular curve generated by a certain value of V_{12}, $V_{12} = V_{12}^0$. Suppose, now, that time elapses and 2's demand, q_2, moves exactly along the curve AB, where the ordinate has become the T-axis instead of the t-axis. This means that 1's expectations are fulfilled and therefore his value of V_{12} will remain unchanged. However, as 2 moves along AB the value of q_2 changes, according to equation (3.7). Thus, 1 will change his own demand q_1 as a result of the direct interdependence, even though his expectations regarding 2's behaviour proved correct. It can be seen that the existence of direct interdependence causes the bargainers' decisions to exhibit inconsistency over time.

It will be taken as axiomatic that a model is unsatisfactory if it involves bargainers making decisions exhibiting inconsistency over time. We make the postulate: in any satisfactory model of the bargaining process, a bargainer does not revise his decision when his expectations are fulfilled.[1] Within the present framework, involving the pure intransigence assumption, this postulate implies that direct interdependence must be absent. If the pure intransigence assumption were relaxed, a bargainer may be planning to change his demand during the future, so that a change of demand could be consistent with his previous decision. However, in the present framework which retains the pure intransigence assumption, this postulate entails that all adjustments must take place via the conjectural interdependence. Bargainer 1's current demand is given by (6.4) which we write as

$$(6.8) \qquad u_i'(q_i) = a_i u_i(q_i) \frac{\partial t_i^*}{\partial q_i}.$$

This does not involve us, as yet, in making any assumptions about the dependence of t_i^* on q_i. We will now show how our

---

[1] This does not mean that a bargainer must not change his demand when his expectations are fulfilled. In a more sophisticated model, without the intransigence assumption, a bargainer may decide to make concessions and it is this decision to concede that would not be revised if his expectations were fulfilled.

previous postulate imposes new constraints on this dependence.

For direct interdependence to be absent, equation (6.8) must be independent of q_j. This condition will be satisfied if $\dfrac{\partial t_i^*}{\partial q_i}$ is independent of q_j. A sufficient condition for this is

(6.9) $$t_i^* = z_i(q_i) + z_j(q_j).$$

(Under reasonable conditions of smoothness this condition is necessary as well as sufficient to ensure that $\dfrac{\partial t_i^*}{\partial q_i}$ is independent of q_j.) The conclusion of this argument is that, within the present framework involving the intransigence assumption, the condition for a bargainer's decisions to exhibit consistency over time is that the t_i^*-function is separable, i.e. can be written in the form given by equation (6.9). (Clearly, Cross's function (3.6) satisfies this condition.) It can be seen, therefore, that it is not the direct interdependence which itself leads to inconsistencies, but its operation in the context of the pure intransigence assumption.

5. AN ILLUSTRATIVE MODEL

In constructing a model it is necessary to seek a t_i^*-function which satisfies not only the conditions (6.1) but also the new condition (6.9). It can easily be shown that the assumption (1.9), for example, gives rise to a t_i^*-function which does not satisfy the new condition.[1] A relatively simple function which would satisfy all the conditions, including the new one, is

(6.10) $$t_i^* = V_{ij}\left\{\frac{1}{(M - q_i)} - \frac{1}{q_j}\right\}.$$

---

[1] Substituting (1.9) into (1.4) with $E_i(T)\{q_i(t)\} = q_i(T)$, we find

$$t_i^* = \frac{V_{ij}(q_i + q_j - M)}{(M - q_i)}$$

which is not a separable function of q_i, q_j.

94

In building a model, the next requirement is a form of expectations which is consistent with this t_i^*-function. That is, we need a form of expectations $E_i(T)\{q_j(t)\}$ which, when it is substituted in (1.4) with $E_i(T)\{q_i(t)\} = q_i(T)$ (representing the intransigence assumption), yields (6.10) as the solution for t_i^*. A relatively simple form of expectations which satisfies this condition is

$$(6.11) \qquad E_i(T)\{q_j(t)\} = \frac{V_{ij}q_j(T)}{tq_j(T) + V_{ij}}$$

which also satisfies the independence assumption since it does not involve q_i. This equation would produce a dependence of expectations on t and V_{ij} of the same form as that shown in Figure 1.5. The shift in the position of the curve as V_{ij} changes would be in the direction shown if $V_{ij}'' > V_{ij}'$. This follows from the fact that

$$(6.12) \qquad \frac{\partial}{\partial V_{ij}} E_i(T)\{q_j(t)\} = \frac{q_j^2 t}{(tq_j + V_{ij})^2}$$

which is greater than 0 when $t > 0$.

The theory of decision-making in this model arises from the application of equation (1.7) to the new assumption (6.10) after substitution in the utility function (6.3), again with the linear assumption $u_i(q_i) = \xi_i q_i$. The theory of adjustments arises from the application of (1.11) to the new assumption (6.11). This then gives rise to the following system of equations.

$$a_i q_i V_{ij} = (M - q_i)^2$$

$$(6.13) \qquad \frac{dV_{ij}}{dT} = \gamma_i \left[\frac{q_i^2}{V_{ij}} + \frac{dq_j}{dT} \right] \qquad \begin{matrix} i = 1,2 \\ j = 1,2 \\ i \neq j \end{matrix}$$

This system of equations proved to be intractable as far as a general solution was concerned. Numerical solutions of the equations for some sets of values of a_1, a_2, γ_1, γ_2, q_1^0, q_2^0[1] were

---

[1] We could alternatively have used a_1, a_2, γ_1, γ_2, V_{12}^0, V_{21}^0, but q_1^0, q_2^0 have more immediate significance than V_{12}^0, V_{21}^0.

calculated on a *KDF9* computer using the fourth order Runge-Kutta-Merson method. These solutions are shown in Table 6.1. Sets 1–4 are all instances of the symmetrical case where $a_1 = a_2$, $\gamma_1 = \gamma_2$, $q_1^0 = q_2^0$ and therefore $\bar{q}_1 = \bar{q}_2$. The remaining sets 5–11 are asymmetrical cases. These results are not intended to give a systematic solution of the system of equations but only an illustrative idea about the workings of the model[1].

	a_1	a_2	γ_1	γ_2	q_1^0	q_2^0	T	$\bar{q}_1$	$\bar{q}_2$
1	0·25	0·25	2·0	2·0	60	60	3·0	50	50
2	0·20	0·20	2·0	2·0	60	60	4·5	50	50
3	0·25	0·25	1·5	1·5	60	60	3·8	50	50
4	0·25	0·25	2·0	2·0	55	55	2·0	50	50
5	0·25	0·25	2·0	2·0	50	70	2·7	46	54
6	0·30	0·25	2·0	2·0	60	60	2·6	48	52
7	0·40	0·25	2·0	2·0	60	60	1·9	46	54
8	0·50	0·25	2·0	2·0	60	60	1·5	44	56
9	0·25	0·25	1·5	2·0	60	60	3·4	51	49
10	0·25	0·25	1·0	2·0	60	60	3·9	53	47
11	0·25	0·25	0·5	2·0	60	60	4·9	55	45

a_i = discounting rate of bargainer i
γ_i = learning rate of bargainer i
q_i^0 = initial demand of bargainer i
T = time taken to reach agreement
$\bar{q}_i$ = outcome for bargainer i

Table 6.1

It is clear that a great deal of work remains to be done in finding systematic numerical solutions and approximate analytical solutions to this model and to models of this type. A fruitful direction for further work might be the investigation of the behaviour of models where the pure intransigence assumption is relaxed and of models of the type discussed in Chapter IV with an asymmetry between the forms of decision

[1] Unfortunately, direct comparisons with the numerical example given by Cross (J. G. Cross, 'A Theory of the Bargaining Process,' *American Economic Review*, 55, 1965, pp. 92–4) cannot be made since the present parameter γ_i is not comparable with Cross's parameter α_i owing to a difference in dimensions. Whereas Cross's α_i has dimensions of [time]$^{-1}$, the parameter γ_i has dimensions which depend on the units of q_1, q_2 as well as on time. For this reason comparisons between the size of α_i and γ_i have no significance.

rule adopted by the bargainers. The obstacles in the path of serious testing of these models would seem to be considerable since sufficiently rich data for this purpose can most likely be obtained only under the highly artificial circumstances involved in gaming experiments.

BIBLIOGRAPHY

ALLEN, R. G. D., *Mathematical Economics*, Macmillan, London, 1959.

BAILEY, M. J., *National Income and the Price Level*, McGraw-Hill, New York, 1962.

BISHOP, R. L., 'Game-Theoretic Analyses of Bargaining,' *Quarterly Journal of Economics*, 77, 1963, pp. 559–602.

——, 'A Zeuthen-Hicks Theory of Bargaining,' *Econometrica*, 32, 1964, pp. 410–17.

BOULDING, K. E., *The Image*, University of Michigan Press, Ann Arbor, 1961.

BOWLEY, A. L., 'On Bilateral Monopoly,' *Economic Journal*, 38, 1928, pp. 651–9.

BURTON, J. W., *International Relations: A General Theory*, Cambridge University Press, Cambridge, England, 1965.

CHAMBERLIN, E. H., *The Theory of Monopolistic Competition*, Harvard University Press, Cambridge, Mass., 1956.

CODDINGTON, A., 'A Theory of the Bargaining Process: Comment,' *American Economic Review*, 56, 1966, pp. 522–30.

——, 'Game Theory, Bargaining Theory and Strategic Reasoning,' *Journal of Peace Research*, Vol. 4, No. 1, pp. 39–45.

COURNOT, A., *Researches into the Mathematical Principles of the Theory of Wealth*, translated by N. T. Bacon, Macmillan, New York, 1897.

CROSS, J. G., 'A Theory of the Bargaining Process,' Ph.D. thesis, Princeton University, Princeton, 1964.

——, 'A Theory of the Bargaining Process,' *American Economic Review*, 55, 1965, pp. 67–94.

DEUTSCH, K. W. *The Nerves of Government*, Free Press of Glencoe, New York, 1963.

EDGEWORTH, F. Y., *Mathematical Psychics*, C. Kegan Paul, London, 1881.

FELLNER, W. J., *Competition Among the Few*, Knopf, New York, 1949.

FOLDES, L., 'A Determinate Model of Bilateral Monopoly,' *Economica*, 122, 1964, pp. 117–31.

GALBRAITH, J. K., *American Capitalism: The Concept of Countervailing Power*, Hamish Hamilton, London, 1957.

HARSANYI, J. C., 'Approaches to the Bargaining Problem before and after the Theory of Games,' *Econometrica*, 24, 1956, pp. 144–57.

HENDERSON, J. M. and R. E. QUANDT, *Microeconomic Theory*, McGraw-Hill, New York, 1958.

Luce, R. D. and H. Raiffa, *Games and Decisions*, J. Wiley & Sons, New York, 1957.

Nash, J. F., 'The Bargaining Problem,' *Econometrica*, 18, 1950, pp. 155–62.

——, 'Two-person Cooperative Games,' *Econometrica*, 21, 1953, pp. 128–40.

Neumann, J. von and O. Morgenstern, *Theory of Games and Economic Behavior*, J. Wiley & Sons, New York, 1964.

Ozga, S. A., *Expectations in Economic Theory*, Weidenfeld and Nicolson, London, 1965.

Parsons, T., *The Social System*, Free Press of Glencoe, New York, 1951.

Pen, J., 'A General Theory of Bargaining,' *American Economic Review*, 42, 1952, pp. 24–42.

——, *The Wage Rate under Collective Bargaining*, translated by T. S. Preston, Harvard University Press, Cambridge, Mass., 1959.

Phillips, A. W., 'Stabilisation Policy in a Closed Economy,' *Economic Journal*, 64, 1954, pp. 290–323.

Rapoport, A., *Fights, Games and Debates*, University of Michigan Press, Ann Arbor, 1960.

Rapoport, A. and Carol Orwant, 'Experimental Games: A Review,' *Game Theory and Related Approaches to Social Behavior*, edited by M. Shubik, J. Wiley & Sons, New York, 1964, Chapter 20.

Rapoport, A. and A. M. Chammah, *Prisoner's Dilemma*, University of Michigan Press, Ann Arbor, 1965.

Rapoport, A., 'Models of Conflict: Cataclysmic and Strategic,' paper presented at the Symposium 'Conflict in Society,' The CIBA Foundation, London, 1965.

Samuelson, P. A., *Foundations of Economic Analysis*, Harvard University Press, Cambridge, Mass., 1961.

Saraydar, E., 'Zeuthen's Theory of Bargaining: A Note,' *Econometrica*, 33, 1965, pp. 802–13.

Schelling, T. C., *The Strategy of Conflict*, Oxford University Press, New York, 1963.

Shackle, G. L. S., *Expectation in Economics*, Cambridge University Press, Cambridge, England, 1949.

——, 'The Nature of the Bargaining Process,' *The Theory of Wage Determination*, edited by J. T. Dunlop, Macmillan, London, 1964, Chapter 19.

Shubik, M., *Strategy and Market Structure*, J. Wiley & Sons, New York, 1959.

Siegel, S. and L. E. Fouraker, *Bargaining and Group Decision Making*, McGraw-Hill, New York, 1960.

Simon, H. A., 'A Behavioral Model of Rational Choice,' *Quarterly Journal of Economics*, 69, 1955, pp. 99–118.

Strotz, R. H., 'Myopia and Inconsistency in Dynamic Utility Maximization,' *Review of Economic Studies*, 23, 1956, pp. 165–80.

Triffin, R., *Monopolistic Competition and General Equilibrium Theory*, Harvard University Press, Cambridge, Mass., 1940.

TUSTIN, A., *The Mechanism of Economic Systems*, Heinemann, London, 1953.

WALTON, R. E. and R. B. MCKERSIE, *A Behavioral Theory of Labor Negotiations*, McGraw-Hill, New York, 1965.

WOLD, H., *Econometric Model Building*, North Holland Publishing Co., Amsterdam, 1964.

ZEUTHEN, F., *Problems of Monopoly and Economic Warfare*, Routledge & Sons, London, 1930.

INDEX

Allen, R. G. D., 54n

Bailey, M. J., 50–51
bargainer, 'Cross-type,' 78–79
bargaining costs, 47, 51, 52
bargaining, exploratory, 82
bargaining, fixed threat, 7, 35
bargaining, hard, 82
bargaining, integrative, 7
bargaining, intra-organisational, 6
bargaining mentality, 91
bargaining power, xiv
bargaining relationship, 69, 80
bargaining skill, xvi
bilateral monopoly, xiii, xiv, xv, 3, 4, 5, 6, 8, 11, 12, 57
Bishop, R. L., 30n, 35n, 41–45, 48, 61, 71n
bluffing, 49
Boulding, K. E., 1
Bowley, A. L., 11
Burton, J. W., 54n

calculus of variations, 62
Chamberlin, E. H., 2n
Chammah, A. M., 69n
closed loops, 49–57
Coddington, A., viii, ix, x, 56n, 81n
conflict, strategic and cataclysmic models of, 79

conjectural interdependence, 12, 86, 92, 93
contract curve, 27
contract zone, viii, 8, 26, 45, 47, 73, 82, 83
convergence in Cross's theory, 46–47
countervailing power, xiv
Cournot, A., 58–60
Cross, J. G., 3, 9, 18, 19, 20, 21, 22, 30n, 44, 45–48, 49–57, 61–62, 63, 64, 81, 82n, 86, 87, 94, 96n

decision rule, level of, defined, 63
decision rule, self-generating, 58
decision rule, self-generating, defined, 60
decision rule, self-replacing, 58, 62, 64, 68, 69
decision rule, self-replacing, defined, 60
decisions, consistency of, ix, 91–94
decisions, consistency of expectations and, 58–60, 63, 69, 91
demand curve, 4–6
Deutsch, K. W., 54n, 56n
discounting, xvii, 42, 47, 66, 77
discounting, assumption of exponential, 51
Dunlop, J. T., 24n

103